G₅

THE BODY
BROKEN

THE BODY
BROKEN

ANSWERING GOD'S CALL
to LOVE ONE ANOTHER

ROBERT BENSON

WATERBROOK
PRESS

THE BODY BROKEN
PUBLISHED BY WATERBROOK PRESS
2375 Telstar Drive, Suite 160
Colorado Springs, Colorado 80920
A division of Random House, Inc.

ISBN 1-4000-7076-7

The Body Broken was originally published in hardcover by Doubleday in
2003.

The Library of Congress has cataloged the hardcover edition as follows:
Benson, R. (Robert), 1952–
    The body broken : answering God's call to love one another /
Robert Benson.
        p. cm.
    ISBN 0-385-50614-7
    1. Benson, R. (Robert), 1952– 2. Christian biography–United States.
        3. Church–Unity. 4. Christian sects. I. Title.
    BR1725.B435A3 2003
    280'.042–dc21   2002041670

Printed in the United States of America
2004–First WaterBrook Press Paperback Edition

10 9 8 7 6 5 4 3 2 1

This book is for Miss Jones,

who keeps telling me that it can be done,

and should be done, and that it matters that I try.

———

And it is, as always,

for the Friends of Silence and of the Poor,

wherever you may be.

CONTENTS

———

If our common life yields anything to stir the heart,

any loving consolation, any sharing of the Spirit,

any warmth of affection or compassion,

fill my cup of happiness by thinking and feeling alike,

with the same love for one another, the same turn of mind,

and a common care for unity.

–SAINT PAUL

———

Never resign yourself

to the scandal of the separation of Christians,

all who so readily confess love for their neighbor,

and yet remain divided.

Be consumed with zeal for the unity of

the Body of Christ.

–THE RULE OF TAIZE

FOREWORD

My first encounter with Robert Benson was as a young musician, attending a seminar for Christian artists and wannabes at a large YMCA camp in the Rocky Mountains. This was a high-profile event where talented Christians put their best foot forward for peers and powers in the music industry, and Robert stuck out like a sore thumb. Here was a small, weak-voiced man putting his worst foot forward seemingly on purpose, and I was riveted by the power of his audacious simplicity.

In a world of hype and hyperbole and a market dominated by result-oriented literature and self-help products, Robert Benson dares to tell us the truth about himself and how he sees the world around him. I have him on a very short list of people who do this well enough to be public with their lives and their thoughts, for they have been a huge inspiration for me, both in my personal life and in my work.

I remember the first time I heard Bob read his material on stage and I thought: *Here is a very brave man.* And I would repeat this assessment after reading *The Body Broken.* For it takes a brave man to go public with his doubts and pains in the context of a highly success-oriented spiritual market. This book will provide no solutions, no steps to fulfillment, no magic formulas to erase the pain, the pressure, or the pounds from your life, but it will warm your heart with memorable stories of ordinary people and it will open your eyes to the truth and the hope found in the midst of life's struggles.

Probably Robert Benson's greatest gift to us comes in the way he cherishes every individual he meets along his journey. In doing so, he tells us more about the image of God than he ever could theologically or philosophically.

In reading Robert Benson, I am reminded of the last lines of the Crowded House hit, "Don't Dream It's Over."

> *There's a battle ahead; many battles are lost,*
> *But you'll never see the end of the road*
> *While you're traveling with me.*

This is Robert Benson's promise to us, too, and I'm glad of it. In a time when bookstores are full of books and films about the end of the road (everyone seems to want to know), *The Body Broken* takes us on a journey for the sake of the journey itself, and in the process, it teaches us about loving one another, not by imperative, but by example. This may be a book you will want to read often, because its power resides not in what it teaches, but in how differently you will see other people after you have seen them through the author's eyes.

But take it slowly, for the prize does not come at the end, it is doled out in small treasures along the way. Go too fast and you most definitely will miss something. I know I have; that's why I'm reading it again.

–JOHN FISCHER, author of *Love Him in the Morning: Reflections on God's Faithfulness*

LOOKING AT THE MYSTERY

You are no longer aliens in a foreign land,

but fellow citizens with God's people,

members of God's own household.

You are being built with all the rest

into a spiritual dwelling for God.

–SAINT PAUL

O God, creator and preserver of all,

we pray especially for thy holy Church:

that it may be so guided and governed by thy good Spirit,

that all who profess themselves Christians

may be led into the way of truth,

and hold the faith in unity of spirit,

in the bonds of peace, and in righteousness of life.

And this we beg for Jesus Christ's sake. Amen.

–THE BOOK OF COMMON PRAYER

ONE OF OUR NEIGHBORS is, by her own description, an old widow woman. Miss Dessie is in her seventies, and she lives next door and she works nights as a maintenance worker in the pediatric ward of one of the hospitals in the city. One of us—my wife, my son, my daughter, or myself—will see her most every day, and we try to be a good enough neighbor to her so she will continue to say what she has said about us a time or two: that "The Lord done sent y'all to me." Which is the sort of thing that she says after we do something like deliver her spare key when she locks herself out, or water her monkey grass when we are watering ours, or mow her lawn when we have our mower out. It is not much for us to do, I admit, but she likes it when we do those things. We are becoming more and more convinced that God sent Miss Dessie to us, if the truth be told.

Because she has to be at the hospital in time for the graveyard shift, she leaves her house in the dark each night about 9:30. She walks the two blocks to the corner just in time to catch a bus that will take her a mile to a place where she waits on another corner for another bus. That one will take her to yet another corner, at which point she gets off and walks the six blocks or so to the hospital. By bus, it can take her more than an hour to make a trip that only takes about ten minutes by car.

We will be coming home from somewhere some evening, and it will be cold or raining or both, and we will see Miss Dessie walking or waiting, and we will run her to work in our car. She used to have a car of her own, but she loaned it to a woman who ran the engine without any oil and the engine died, and now the car sits useless in Miss Dessie's driveway between her house and ours. It may be better that way, because I am not convinced that Miss Dessie is tall enough to see over the steering wheel anyway. Once or twice we have tried to organize a rotating carpool among the neighbors to drive her to work, but she is resistant to being that dependent on anyone.

One night, as we were driving her to work, we told Miss Dessie how much we worried about her out in the dark, walking through streets that can still be something less than friendly in the neighborhoods between here and the hospital. We asked her if she was ever afraid.

"No, no," she said. "I just pull my front door to and lock it up and turn around at the top of the steps and say, 'I am washed in the blood of the Lamb.' And then I just go on down the steps." Evidently, that is all that it takes for her to be ready to go out into the dark and not be afraid.

More than once, I have found myself wishing that I

could see God and my relationship to God in the same pure and simple way that Miss Dessie does.

✦✦✦✦✦✦✦

A few years ago, the nice quiet life in the suburbs that my wife and I had fashioned for just the two of us came to an end. My two teenage children came to live with us, so we moved from one part of the city to another so that we could be nearer to certain schools and particular friends and close cousins.

That's when we ended up in Miss Dessie's neighborhood, which is just five minutes or so from the heart of the city, one of the old trolley car neighborhoods that had been carved out of a huge farm during the decades just before and after the First World War. It is full of Victorian cottages with front porches that people sit on in good weather, and sidewalks that people walk on every day, and pocket-size front yards that are suitable for greeting your neighbors across as you take your evening stroll. There is a small grocery a few blocks away and a coffeehouse just down the street, and there is a place to buy plants, a place to buy gifts, and a good restaurant all within walking distance. We are only about five to ten minutes from everything we really love in the city—our favorite bookstores and art galleries and restaurants and the cathedral where we worship. We only have to use the freeway when we are running late to the airport or have to go out of town. About three times a week, one of us wonders aloud why we did not move here years ago. Our neighborhood is not the only gift that came our way when the children moved in with us, but it is in the top five or so whenever we think of the gifts that my children have brought our way.

As time has gone by, we have become more and more involved in the neighborhood association, and the next thing that I knew, I was living with the newsletter lady. I was already married to her, but now that she is the editor of the newsletter, she happens to know nearly everyone in the neighborhood, who is coming and who is going, and I have more friends than I have ever had in my life, not many of whom are like me in many respects.

In the thirty or so square blocks that we call home, there are people of every color and every cultural background that you can name, as well as some that I have yet to figure out. There is a mosque and a Catholic church and a Missionary Baptist church and a Greater Christ Temple, whatever denomination that is. There are accountants and talent managers and bartenders and property appraisers and schoolteachers and a man who delivers groceries to old people. He calls them old people, though he is old enough to be sharing his house these days with a son-in-law who retired fifteen years ago. There are also alcoholics and drug dealers and kids who are going to get into terrible trouble if they are not luckier in the next few years than they seem to have been in their first few. There is a community center and a city park and a bakery and a pair of convenience markets, one of which closes before dark and the other of which I am afraid to visit after dark. There are people who have been here all their lives, and people who once lived here then moved away and have since come back. There are folks moving in and out of here all the time. It reminds me of the Church.

CRITICAL

A man whose last name is Thomas is one of the people who lives close by. He is a writer and a musician and a minister, and he is bright and funny and thoughtful. By his own humorous admission, he has been put on the planet to tell everyone exactly how they are to live. We have a running joke between us that I am the guy to call if you are certain about everything spiritual, because I can raise more doubts (generally out of my own experience) than anyone that either one of us has ever met. And I can do so in less time than anyone that you will ever meet.

He, on the other hand, can quote enough scripture and posit enough theological and intellectual truths to straighten you out and eliminate all your doubts, setting you on the road to glory—it will take only about ten minutes or so. All that is required is that you do exactly as he says and believe exactly as he believes and never ask any more questions. I am the Doubting Thomas and he is the Answer Thomas, and we both grin whenever we think of each other.

Among the other things that he does is to pastor a small community of people. They worship together each week in a meeting room in a nearby hotel. They come from all sorts of places in their journeys and they tend toward the artistic and also toward the evangelical. They have been together long enough now that they have their own baseball cap with a logo, have started to think about buying an old building in which to worship, and have begun to do work among the poor together. They invited me to read from some of my work at their Christmas service last year and so I went. It made me nervous to be so full of questions myself while standing in front of people who seem so sure about some of the things that I am struggling so hard to understand and believe, but I decided that one should be very careful about turning down invitations from a guy known as the Answer Thomas.

They were as sweet and kind and generous to me that evening as any group of people has ever been. The experience made me want to look at God through the same window that they are looking through, in the hopes that I could become as sweet and kind and generous myself, even if I cannot ever become quite as certain as they are.

I have spent my whole life around Christian people of one stripe or another. I was raised in the Nazarene church, then I became a Methodist, and now I am an Episcopalian. Because of the work that I have done, first as a religious music publisher and now as a writer of books about Christian spirituality, I have spent a fair amount of time with people from all across the spectrum of Christian theology, doctrine, and practice. You name the group, and some of them are sure to be people that I know by name. I have worshiped with them, argued with them, prayed with them, done business with them, wept with them, and laughed with them. I have been to retreats and conferences, camp meetings and mission trips, Bible studies and revivals, festive Eucharists and Jesus festivals. I have been a fellow pilgrim and seeker and traveling companion with one crowd or another of them for as long as I can remember.

Church folks have loved me, supported me, comforted me, and challenged me throughout my days in ways that have made me what I am, for better or for worse. I hope and pray that remains true for me for the rest of my life. But from time to time, that same crowd has broken my heart. I expect that I have returned the favor a time or two as well, I am afraid.

"We Christians can be awfully hard on each other," said my friend Reuben Welch once. "We are especially hard on each other when it comes to the things that matter the most. And we can be just as hard on each other about the things that matter the least."

⚂⚃⚂⚃⚂⚃⚂

When I was attending a class in anticipation of becoming a Methodist, the Methodist pastors taught me a way of looking at the different ways that different parts of the Church see the journey of faith. They drew a big rectangle up on a blackboard and called it the Wesley Quadrilateral. When I became an Episcopalian some years later, it was pointed out to me that this diagram was really known as the Anglican Quadrilateral. They said the Methodists had gotten it from

John Wesley and that he lived and died an Anglican priest, not a Methodist. (It turns out Martin Luther never gave up being a Catholic priest, either, though it is hard to get many Lutherans or Catholics to say so.)

Whoever it belongs to, the Quadrilateral is a tool used to discern the different ways that we look at the Mystery that is God. At one corner is scripture, at another corner is experience. In a third corner is reason, and in the fourth corner is tradition. These corners are bound together with God in the center, it is the Mystery, the mysterious presence of the Almighty, that fills out the space in between.

Think of the four corners as large windows, so to speak, through which groups of people are looking in order to catch a glimpse of the Mystery itself. Certain groups look primarily through certain windows: Catholics rely heavily on the view through the window of tradition, while Baptists look more through the window called scripture. Pentecostals, with their emphasis on the work of the Holy Spirit, spend a fair amount of time looking through the window called experience, while Unitarians focus on the one marked reason. Though none of us, either as groups or individuals, are likely to be found looking only through one window, our primary points of view are pretty clear.

One realizes pretty quickly that no one window affords a view of the entire Mystery itself. One can also say that in the course of one's own journey, one has looked through different windows and different combinations of windows. More and more, in my journey, I have come to see the Quadrilateral as a circle. And more and more I come to recognize friends and strangers as they move around the circle—as they are led by God to see the Mystery from a different vantage point.

I began my journey as a Nazarene, and my early years were spent in search of a glimpse of the Mystery through the window of a personal experience with Jesus that I could feel and believe in. As time went on, my knowledge of the scriptures grew, and my view through that particular window began to shape and confirm my sense of who God is and how God can be seen and heard. Then, at a given moment in my journey, I fell in with the Methodists and began to learn about the ancient traditions of the Church that had not been made known to me when I was younger. There was less emphasis on personal experience in this group, but there was also the discovery of the meaning and practice of the sacraments and the liturgy. The next step in my journey moved me to the Anglican communion, at which point my immersion in the traditions of the Church began to deepen. I also began to discover a new way to wrestle with scripture itself, relying more and more on reason, principally through a deeper study of the biblical scholarship of the past fifty years or so.

It is tempting for me to say that I have traveled the perfect road to a well-rounded faith. In reality—and this is one of the few things that I am sure of—it is only my own road to faith. It is similar to the journey that others have made, it is the exact opposite of some, but it is certainly not a prescription. It is simply the way that God has drawn me and led me and looked back at me through the windows over the years.

Another thing that I have become sure of, regardless of

the amount of evidence to the contrary, is that whichever window we are looking through, we have far more in common than we often think that we do. The things that keep Christians apart from other Christians are not nearly so important to me these days as are the things that bind us to one another. It is curious how we seem to talk so much about the former and pay so little attention to the latter.

Three or four blocks north and a block or two east of us, there lives a young man who was recently ordained. He and I have a couple of things in common in addition to the neighborhood, and we talk from time to time about our journeys and the things that we have in common.

Over coffee one day, he told me about his upcoming ordination, about how the service would be conducted in the tradition of his church, and who was going to be there. He named the parts of the service and described who would do what, as well as what words were to be said. He was in tears by the time that he finished, and so was I, just in anticipation for him. He invited me to the ceremony, but I had to be on the road. When the day came, I was hundreds of miles away. I was disappointed that I could not be there with him.

When I returned to town, I asked him how it had gone. He started to describe the moment when the deacons and clergy and such came to the altar to lay their hands upon him for prayer as a sign of the passing of the apostolic mantle from all the generations of clergy—from Saint Peter on down—to him. Then he talked about feeling the weight of the hands on his shoulders as the community that he serves came forward to lay their hands on him as well, as a sign of their acceptance of his calling and his work among them and as a way of blessing him as his journey took this new turn.

It had touched him so deeply that he could hardly talk about it. And that, in turn, touched me so deeply that I could hardly stand to hear him talk about it either. I was grateful that I had gazed through the window of such traditions for a time, long enough at least to have a sense of what he was talking about, and long enough to recognize and remember my own encounters with the Holy that had taken place while looking through the window of the ancient traditions of the Church.

⊠⊠⊠⊠⊠⊠

I have a friend who has a propensity for calling my house at odd hours, and whenever my caller i.d. identifies that he is the one calling, I never answer the phone. The messages are too good to pass up.

"Robert, Robert, Robert," he breathlessly said once. And then in the voice that could not belong to anyone else on the planet, he identified himself. "This is W. G. Henry, in living color." Then came the good part.

"And I have called to tell you, Robert, that I was talking to God this very morning and your very name came up and arrangements have been made especially for you to hear from God today and it will be good. I love you. 'Bye."

W. G. is a Methodist pastor, and although I am certain that he has a first name and a middle name, whatever they are, he is not telling.

"Everything in your life," he said on the first day that I met him, "every book, every sermon, every telephone call, every doubt, every prayer–everything that has ever happened to you–has conspired to bring you to this very moment and this very place among these very people to hear what God has to say to you today." Of all the conspiracy theories that I have ever heard, this is the only one that I believe in.

❦

When I was growing up in the Nazarene church, I had the good fortune to get to know and get to listen to a better than average thinker and preacher named Reuben. His way of opening up the meaning of the scriptures–honest, direct, poetic, rigorous–opened my heart to the scriptures themselves. It gave me a lifelong hunger for preaching that was as full of art and power as it was full of passion and theology, which made it possible for me to be able to really hear Russell when the time came.

In the way that has happened to many people, I was away from my hometown and from my home church for some years in my late twenties. When I eventually wandered back to Nashville and then wandered back into a church, it was into a Methodist church. About two minutes into Russell's first sermon, I knew that I was in a place that could become home for me. He was a brilliant writer of sermons, as good as Reuben, and I stayed in that church for years because of Russell. I stayed long enough to begin to learn about the liturgy and the sacraments, long enough to begin to wonder about the other traditions of Christian prayer and worship that had not been taught to me when I was young, long enough to learn that there were windows into the Mystery that I had not looked through.

Then Russell introduced to me to Ben, and Ben introduced me to the practices of Christian contemplative prayer. Ben is a professor of religion and philosophy at a Southern Baptist university. How he found out about contemplative prayer, I do not know. But the things that he taught me and the places that he showed me prepared my heart for the seeds that began to grow in my heart when I met Brennan, a former Catholic monk.

There are more steps along my journey, more twists and turns in this conspiracy, too many to name here. There is a small army of good people who have been in on it. There is Danny and Father Ed and on and on, including W. G.

If someone had not introduced me to Reuben the Nazarene all those years ago, then my heart would not have been ready when it was time for me to meet Russell the Methodist. So then I would have missed Ben the Baptist and then Brennan the Catholic. If there had been no Brennan in my life, then there would be no Danny and no W. G. and no Father Ed, and maybe, just maybe, no Robert.

This strange crowd, many of whom do not know anyone else in the circle, and others who are named only in the secrets of my heart, as an old prayer goes, came from places on all sides of the Quadrilateral, and they are the ones who kept inviting me in, welcoming me to walk alongside them for a time, encouraging me and helping me to see the Mystery through the window that they were looking through. In the process, they helped me to see more clearly the One Who made us, the One Who came among us, and the One Who will sustain us and lead us into all truth.

I am certain now that my journey would have been poorer had I never been invited to look into any of the windows of the Mystery other than the one that I had always known and always held dear.

⋇⋇⋇⋇⋇⋇

The restaurant in our neighborhood has turned out to be one of the best restaurants in town. It draws people from all over the city, gets written up in national magazines, and is doing very well. Its success matters to us a lot, because we who live here count on it as a kind of second kitchen and gathering place, a place to invite our friends. We want it to prosper.

It is a very sophisticated place, generally full of hip and refined people. (Plus the rest of us.) It is very much a big city sort of place, and the menu has a lot of stuff that my palate cannot always measure up to. My father used to say that he felt as though the whole world was a tuxedo and he was a pair of brown shoes. I used to feel like that when I would go through the door. But now whenever we go through the door, it takes a few minutes to get to the place where we like to sit. It takes a few minutes because we have to wade through a crowd of people who know us by name, and we have to stop to swap hugs and greetings and jokes. Then the people who own the place and the people who work there throw their arms around us or wave at us and say nice things. It is a chore, but we have to stop for that, too. People from the restaurant have been known to show up at my kids' sporting events or cook huge meals in the neighborhood on their days off and invite piles of people, and they give gifts to my wife without any occasion. They never meet a stranger; instead, they welcome everyone with the warmth that you expect from a family.

I do not know exactly how to describe what window they are looking through in order to see into the Mystery—religion is not something that we have talked about a lot—but I know enough to know that they have glimpsed the God of hospitality somewhere. I can only hope that if I keep hanging around them that I will learn to do the same.

◆◆◆◆◆◆◆

"Enter any house that will welcome you," said the One Who came among us, "share their meal, tend their sick, and there is where you will find the kingdom."

More and more I see my own work as that of a host of some sort, setting up tables and pulling up chairs by way of the books that I am given to write and the retreats that I am allowed to lead. I want to keep welcoming people in, hanging up coats and handing out refreshments, if you will. And all the while, I am to be introducing people to others, other travelers and pilgrims who have been looking through one window or another for a while and who are now perhaps bound for some new vantage point. I keep trying to be sure that Ben meets Ed, that Ed meets Danny, that Danny tells his story to Russell, that Russell knows how to get hold of Reuben, and that Reuben has had a chance to visit with W. G.

Whichever window we are looking through now, whichever window we are traveling toward, there are those who have traveled that way before. And because none of us can see the entire Mystery at any given time, what we have to offer each other matters a great deal. Those who believe in and care deeply about and are burning with zeal for the unity of the Body of Christ, as Brother Roger of Taize put it, need to keep setting tables and welcoming others in and hanging up coats and making introductions. Some portion of the Body must be about the business of making conversation that can unite us rather than divide us. Some of us must become courageous enough to look through other windows, and some must become gracious enough to respect the windows that we have not yet looked through. All of us must become more aware that the window that we love is not the only window.

❧❧❧❧❧❧❧

My friend Reuben once said, "Sure, people need Jesus, but most of the time, what they really need is for someone to be Jesus to them."

We who call ourselves by the name Christian are to be the Body of Christ in this world. We are to be Jesus. I expect that it will take the efforts of all of us together, no matter which window we happen to be looking through at a given moment in time. If the Christ is to appear incarnate in this world in these days, then it will be because we are Jesus to other people. Most of us understand that, many of us even say it to each other and to ourselves from time to time. However, there is a terrible truth at work here in our world, in our Church. We are very often incapable of being Jesus to other Christians, which leaves me to wonder how it is we can be confident that we can be Christ to someone outside the Church.

I have hope that we may yet, as the old prayer says, "become one with Christ and one with each other," but I think that will only be true if we tell each other our stories and ask each other our questions. Some of our stories involve things that no one wants to say or to hear about the crowd of people that we refer to as the Body of Christ. Some stories involve pain and hurt, even though they describe events that took place a long time ago. Some of them may be difficult because none of us, including me, want to entertain the notion that we are participating, even if unknowingly, in the daily dismemberment of the very Body that we claim to be. Finally, some of those stories may well suggest that we need to learn to be different people–to be different in the way that we treat each other.

On a fine summer day not too long ago, there was an afternoon game at the local minor league ballpark. (Another of the top five advantages of our neighborhood is that the ball-park is just five minutes away.) As it turned out, a fair number of our neighbors turned up for the ball game, and as the game wore on, we began to discover each other in the stands. We finally ended up all sitting together down in the front two or three rows.

When the game was over, one conversation led to another and the impromptu gathering ended up with a couple grills going in our backyard. Then some people who were out for a walk saw the crowd and decided to drop by to sit and eat and talk for a while. People were coming and going in and out of our house, the breeze was blowing and the sun was setting, the laughter was contagious, and the talk was warm and bright and holy, I think.

All of our neighbors were not there that day—it takes a neighborhood yard sale to turn them all up—but we were approaching a quorum. The Answer Thomas was there and the hospitality folks, too, and the doubter and the rationalists and one or two of about everything in between. For a moment, though, we were as one, telling our stories and listening to those of others. We shared a glimpse of the Mystery in a way that happens from time to time, when strangers and fellow pilgrims gather up in peace, share a meal, and tell their stories, thus becoming something larger together for a few moments.

It reminded me of what the Church is supposed to be. It reminded me of what we might become if we remembered that what binds us is not the particular window we are looking through, for we are seeing as through a glass darkly anyway. What binds us together is not the knowledge that the view through one window or the other is the most correct one. What binds us together is the fact that we are looking at all, seeking a glimpse of the Mystery itself, the Mystery that holds those corners together, the Mystery that can make us one.

2

LET US STAND AND SAY
WHAT WE BELIEVE

Through faith you are all children of God, baptized into union with Christ, and so heirs by promise. There are no divisions, you are all one person in Christ.

–SAINT PAUL

.

Lord of all power and might,
who art the author and giver of all good things:
Graft in our hearts the love of thy Name;
increase in us true religion, nourish us with all goodness,
and bring forth in us the fruit of good works;
through Jesus Christ our Lord,
who liveth and reigneth with thee and the Holy Spirit,
one God forever and ever. Amen.

–THE BOOK OF COMMON PRAYER

WHEN I WAS A KID, my best three buddies and I all went to the same elementary school, learned to play baseball at the same Little League park, ate ice cream at the same Dairy Queen, were charter members of the same chapter of the Fellowship of Christian Athletes that met at our high school, and years later graduated on the same day from that same high school. We also went to different churches together.

Rick was a Southern Baptist, while I was raised in the Church of the Nazarene. Larry was a United Methodist, and Nick grew up in the Church of Christ, not the United Church of Christ but the un-united one, the fundamentalist variety that you find here in the southern states where I have lived for most of my life.

The four of us were pretty much inseparable by the time we got to high school. Looking back on it now, it occurs to me that we may well have been inseparable because not many of the other kids liked us. We were so serious and so straitlaced and so certain. We never fought much over anything at all—not girls, money, grades, sports, not anything, really—except, of course, our religion.

All four of us grew up in fairly devout homes, and our families spent a lot of time at our respective churches. Religion was an important part of our lives, and because it was, we used to compare notes a lot. It seemed important for us to establish for certain which of us was following the true Christian faith and which of us were not. We were experts, as only adolescents can be, on the basic tenets of the Christian faith as held dear by each of our respective denominations, especially the key elements of the faith that most deeply affected high school students in the sixties, particularly kids who lived in suburban homes with two cars, a barbecue pit, brothers and sisters, and most of the important parts of the American Dream firmly in place.

Rick's Southern Baptist faith included these deep and time-honored beliefs: They took Communion three times a year or so, and its proper name was the Lord's Supper; smoking and drinking and dancing were okay, though everyone felt better about it if you would do so out of the sight of other Baptists; baptism was a full body-drenching affair, generally reserved for adults only; the choir sang hymns on Sunday, accompanied by a piano and an organ and led by a minister of music who invariably wore white shoes and a matching belt; and a profession of faith was correctly made and thereby acceptable in the sight of God by going down to the front of the sanctuary and whispering in the pastor's ear while he stood in front of the pulpit at the end of the service, and then he held his arm around you and announced your name to the crowd.

At Larry's church, the First United Methodist Church, they did not take the Lord's Supper. They took the *Eucharist* once each month and from time to time on special days; smoking and drinking and dancing were okay (they even had dances once or twice a year—downstairs in the basement of the church no less); baptism was a sprinkling affair that happened when you were a baby and, as at least one of the four of us was always quick to point out, were too young to even know what was going on; the choir sang *church music* accompanied by an organ; and one made a single profession of faith, once for all time, about the time that you turned thirteen, and it took place in the middle of a service called confirmation.

The members of the Church of Christ were different from the rest. At Nick's church, they took the Lord's Supper every Sunday; they did not smoke or drink or dance, or even laugh very often as I recall; baptisms were held at a nearby river; musical instruments were considered worldly, therefore everything was sung a cappella; and a profession of faith was not necessary, as everyone who went there seemed to have been handpicked by God to begin with. From time to time, one of them would backslide and do something terrible, like become a Nazarene.

At our church, we took Communion once or twice each year whether we needed it or not; smoking and drinking and dancing, and movies for that matter, were all taboo; baptism was a get-your-clothes-wet event that took place in a big pool behind the choir loft, and you could do it any time you chose, the most common being when you came back from a youth retreat all fired up to follow Jesus; the choir sang hymns and gospel songs and praise choruses to a piano and an organ, and trumpets and drums, too, on special occasions; and a profession of faith could be made at the front of the church at the end of a service, but you had to have been on your knees, crying and confessing for a while first, then after you prayed through, which is what it was called, you could be called upon to stand up and testify to everyone as to what a bad guy you had been and how you were back on the road to glory.

Any discussion among the four of us about those perceived bedrock elements of the faith could be counted on to set off an argument as to the state of the particular souls in question. Wherever two or three of us were gathered, someone got painted into a theological corner. We knew we were Christians by how mad we could make each other.

Twenty years later, I had been doing some backsliding of my own, some would say. I prefer to think of it as sliding sideways. I was becoming a Methodist. My high school friend Larry would have been proud, I suppose.

In the eighties, I found myself in the third row on the gospel side of the West End United Methodist Church, just up the road from the church that I was a part of when I was younger. I was discovering and learning and trying to understand what this more formal and sacramental and liturgical way of worshiping means. Because I grew up in the

Nazarene tradition, a tradition that not only did not rely on the ancient liturgy for worship but was even slightly suspicious of it as I recall, all of the Methodist service was new to me. I was falling in love with it week after week after week, even the parts of it that I did not yet understand.

Some new thing—new to me at least—that was part of the ancient worship tradition of the Church seemed to come to my attention each time that I was gathered up with the others in that place.

One day, it was the processional of the ministers and the choir as they came in following the cross from the rear of the sanctuary before worship began; another day, it was being invited to come and kneel at the altar for the Eucharist instead of having it passed through the congregation. One day, it was watching as the minister ceremoniously came halfway up the center aisle to read the gospel lesson aloud in the midst of us; another day, it was reciting the words of the baptismal covenant along with the parents of a child who was being baptized. One day, it was the words of the prayer that we all said aloud together before we were served Communion; another day, it was noticing the way you fold your hands to make a cross when you are being served the Body of Christ.

And on and on and on, week after week, a new discovery coming to me almost every Sunday. As time went by, I began to ask questions and to read books, trying to find out what those movements and gestures and symbols and words meant, where they came from, and what their use meant to me when I was gathered up for worship with the others in church.

"Let us stand and say together what we believe," came the voice of the minister at West End after the sermon one Sunday morning. It was a deep voice, and gentle, too, rich and rolling and practiced, an eastern Kentucky hill country voice. It was the voice of a fine liturgist and preacher, a voice that one might hire to read for a recording of the scriptures or stories or some such thing. I had heard him say the same thing after he finished the sermon for weeks, but on that day, for no reason that was apparent to me at the time or even now, his words quickened my spirit.

"Let us stand and say together what we believe." And so we stood.

"We believe in one God, the Father, the Almighty, maker of heaven and earth, of all that is, seen and unseen," we all said together. And that morning, I began to wonder if it was really true.

What we were saying was the Nicene Creed, an ancient statement of faith of the Church that dates back to the fourth century. Its words were vaguely familiar to me, even though we did not say it very often, if at all, in the Nazarene Church.

Over time, I have come to know other things about the way that the creed is used or not used in different parts of the Church. Some of us say it every Sunday, or another one like it, the Apostles' Creed. Some denominations include it in the back of their hymnals and say it from time to time on particular Sundays for particular reasons. Other groups say it not at all. At least one group who does not say it will tell you that they have no creed but Christ, and I understand that belief as well.

But I also have to say that it if you work your way through the creed line by line, most Christians, even those who are not familiar with the creed itself and the way that it has been used over the years, will say that they believe in the things that are stated in the creed. It is a remarkable statement of the foundational beliefs of the Christian faith.

Some of what I began to wonder that particular Sunday morning as I stood with the others to say what I believed, and still wonder from time to time if the truth be told, had to do with me. Did I, in fact, believe in one God, the Father Almighty? Did I believe in Jesus Christ as the only Son of God? Then there are all the other things in the creed as well: the virgin birth, the death on the cross, the resurrection, the life of the world to come. Was I capable indeed, I wondered, of saying those things out loud with the others week after week, Sunday after Sunday? Was I saying them not simply because I was being asked to but because I actually believed them? Because that was what I was being asked to do.

One Sunday I noticed the "we" part as well. Because if we—all of us in our various and sundry sanctuaries all over Christendom—truly believe these things and hold them in common, then should not some things be different about the way that we treat each other?

And then one day while I was saying the creed, I thought of my high school friends.

Rick was pretty sure that at least two of us were bound for hell, though he never said which two. Larry the Methodist seemed uncertain that there even was a hell. Nick had been taught at the Church of Christ that the other three of us were definitely lost. I had far too much guilt of my own to worry about anyone else's eternal fate. My Southern Baptist girl-friend had taught me how to dance, and so I considered my-self doomed unless I were to get lucky and happen to be at the altar when the trumpet sounded and the roll was called up yonder.

My buddies and I would spend our weekdays in each other's company, going to class, playing ball, talking about girls, trying to get out of algebra, and never arguing about anything except our religion. On Sundays, we would each go off to our respective churches and tell our Sunday school teachers how hard it was for us to follow Jesus at school be-cause we were surrounded by heathens. Then on Mondays, we would be back at school together, spending most of our time with three other guys who were trying just as hard to follow Jesus, and we would go back to arguing about who was following him correctly enough to make it to the prom-ised land.

The arguments usually started up right after the Fellow-ship of Christian Athletes (FCA) prayer meeting before school and were instigated by the leader–often one of us four–having sung or said or read or borne witness to some-thing that raised our theological hackles.

We were not the only four guys in the FCA; there were others. Even though we did not know them as well as we knew each other, we hung around with most of them a bit because all of us played on one team or another for the school. Some of them were Lutheran or Presbyterian or

Catholic. At least one was gay, as it turned out, and another became a big-time rock-and-roll star, another committed suicide, and another was an agnostic, or so he said. I think he came to the FCA meetings and hung around us just to make us nuts. Saint Paul had his thorn in the flesh and we had Walter. Now that I am older, I cannot remember what the four of us said about those outside our little group. I am glad that I cannot remember, too, because I am embarrassed just thinking about how embarrassing what we must have said must have been. We could barely envision enough room on the train to glory for each other, the ones who were most like us. Those who were different, *really* different, would have been considered beyond the pale for sure, and we probably did not hesitate, in our self-righteousness, to say so.

I do not go to the Methodist church any longer, I have now become an Episcopalian. I am not so sure what Larry or either of my other two high school friends would think about that. Maybe they would just be glad that somebody took me in.

There are Sunday mornings now, after the sermon has been read and it is time for us to stand and say the creed, time to stand and say what we believe, that I find myself struck by the great power and majesty of the ideas and beliefs that are held in those words.

"We believe in one God . . . incarnate . . . resurrection . . . one holy Church . . . the resurrection of the dead . . . the life of the world to come. . . ." I am in awe of those words, and I still wonder if I can possibly hold them in my head and in my heart with anything that resembles real devotion. "I believe, help thou my unbelief," I always want to say at the end.

"Wherever we go, there seems to be only one business at hand," wrote Annie Dillard, "that of finding workable compromises between the sublimity of our ideas and the absurdity of the fact of us."

Once in a while, I find myself thinking of the absurdity of the facts of me and of my lifelong struggle to lay those facts down next to the sublimity of the ideas in the creed that I say each week. But I have to confess that I think about us all that way from time to time. "We believe in one God . . . one Lord, Jesus Christ" is what faithful people are saying in other churches, even as we are saying it in ours. Sometimes they are using a different creed, sometimes their community has found other words and other ways to make the same statements, but we are all saying it somehow.

I wonder if we think or know or remember that others mean their stated creeds in those other churches. I wonder if we even realize or contemplate the fact that the others are saying such things. I wonder if it ever reminds us that we are brothers and sisters of the household of faith.

⊠⊠⊠⊠⊠⊠

I have not spoken to Rick or Larry or Nick since graduation. I expect they may see each other from time to time because I heard they all still lived in the same small town in which we grew up, but I do not know for sure. I am afraid that when we went our separate ways back then, each one of us was absolutely convinced that the other three did not have a clue about what it meant to really follow Jesus. We had been so busy arguing about the details that we missed at least one of the larger portions of the point.

I know that it is funny to look back and laugh at the collective schoolboy ignorance that my friends and I displayed, but I have to say that it is not funny when grown-ups do such things—and we still do. We still argue over details, but that is not the worst part. The worst part is that we do not know the core tenets of our faith as well as we might.

We do not always hold our faith dear the way that we should. We do not always wrestle and struggle with our beliefs as though they really mattered. We are not always quick to hold the way that we live our lives up into the light of the sublimity of our ideas. We do not always realize the potential of those ideas to make us truly one with Christ and one with each other and one with the saints, and one with our own sweet selves, for that matter. What we do seem to hold dear is the absurdity of fighting over who has figured out the way to be more theologically correct than others who are trying to follow Jesus as well.

If I had it to do over again, and I do not—which is not so bad since we are talking about high school here, and once is certainly enough—I know how I would now lead off the FCA meeting every time it would be my turn to do so. In fact, when I think of my friends now, I wish that we could meet together, along with the others who would join us in the back of the lunchroom in those few minutes before school began all those years ago.

"Let us stand and say together what we believe," I would say. And then, in a better voice than that skinny little one that I had back in those days, I would lead us along: "We believe in one God, the Father, the Almighty, maker of heaven and earth . . ."

It would be a better way to begin a day spent trying to to follow Jesus than arguing over the things that we argued about back then. It would be at least a way to remind us of what binds us together, to provide a glimpse of our faith as something larger and deeper and broader than just the little world in which we live.

3

IN SPIRIT AND IN TRUTH

All who are moved by the spirit of God

are the children of God.

–SAINT PAUL

O Almighty God, who pours out on all who desire it

the spirit of grace and of supplication:

Deliver us, when we draw near to thee,

from coldness of heart and wanderings of mind,

that with steadfast thoughts and kindled affections,

we may worship thee in spirit and in truth;

through Jesus Christ our Lord. Amen.

–THE BOOK OF COMMON PRAYER

I HAVE ONLY THE ONE PHOTOGRAPH, and I have not looked at it in years. I do not have to. The memory of how I looked in 1967 is, unfortunately, forever etched in my mind. Most of the other photographic evidence is, hopefully, lost in an attic somewhere.

It is a black-and-white photograph of about sixteen of us kids from church. We are stretched out in a line across the top of a hill, trying as hard as we can to look like a rock-and-roll band.

What we really were was a youth group that had turned ourselves into a musical group. We were young, we rehearsed enough together to be called a group, and I recall that at least two of us were musical. That seemed to be enough in those early days of Christian rock and roll, so off we went. We used to spend a part of our summers traveling from church to church, striking terror into the hearts of the saints every time we plugged in our electric guitars and set up our drums. Just to be safe, we took a preacher with us; he would say a few words and offer a prayer and an altar call at the end, so that the local pastor could say that everyone had been to church, no matter how much damage we had done before the preacher preached.

My father was pretty well known as a speaker, and most of the people who heard my father speak thought that he got his start working at retreats and colleges, or that one year he had sprung fully formed onto the stage in front of the large crowds that he spoke to at one religious event or another in the last few years of his life.

But he actually got his start as a traveling speaker by rescuing our church's traveling youth group. After an hour or so of whatever it was that we did in the name of making a joyful noise, he would get up and do whatever it was that he did to bring some measure of decorum to the proceedings.

Much of the time, our assault on the musical and worship sensibilities of some poor unsuspecting congregation made the congregation itself pretty nervous. We were often too loud or too different or too undignified for some folks. In the sixties, a fair amount of grown-ups were generally afraid of their children a fair amount of the time, whether they were in the Church or without it. The children of the sixties were afraid themselves, I think.

But we didn't scare anybody on the night we visited the Biltmore Holiness Temple.

As loud and raucous as we were by the standards of the Nazarene churches that we usually worked in, we were barely adequate warm-up material for the folks who had gathered up for church on the Sunday evening that we played at the Biltmore Holiness Temple.

The evening started out normally enough, and the people were a more generous audience than usual as I recall. But something that we said or sang during the hour or so that we were performing must have been moving to someone, because a few of the people in the pews decided that they needed to stand up and move around a little. One or two of them started dancing in the aisles, and then one man stood up on the pew and began to sing along. He was clearly singing his own song while we were trying to sing ours, an enthusiastic descant, one might say. But he was singing it in a tongue that none of us—visitor or member—had ever heard before and maybe since. One woman collapsed on the floor in front of us, and several others just stood in their places with their hands in the air as they began to shout.

In our local Nazarene church, there would be times when the same sorts of things would happen in the worship services. They did not happen a lot, but they were frequent enough that we had some idea of what such expressions of joy and worship were about.

Then the organ began to play, which was a little unsettling because none of us in the group played the organ, and none of us wanted to turn around to see who was playing. A man joined our group and borrowed one of our guitars, another sat down at the drums, which had recently been abandoned by our drummer, who had fled for a seat in the front row next to my father. The congregation proceeded to sing their own set of songs.

At that, most of us just sat down where we were stand-ing, apprehensive about what we were seeing and what might take place next. We had heard older people in our church freely express their faith, but this was a good deal more intense, to say the least. Some of us scattered, seek-ing out shelter next to the adults who had traveled along with us.

After an hour or so, the crowd began to calm down and become quiet again, returning to their places. In the midst of this, the local pastor gave my father a signal of some sort, and my father stood up and spoke for a few minutes, then we sang two more songs, someone said a prayer over us all, and the service was over.

In the bus on the way to our hotel, I asked my father if he had any idea that what had happened was going to happen or if he even knew what it all meant. He explained it to me, I expect, or as well as he could and as well as a fifteen-year-old could understand it. This is the part that I have never forgotten: "If they had not done that," he said, "those folks would not have felt like they had been to church."

❦❦❦❦❦❦

I grew up as the oldest son and frequent traveling compan-ion of a well-traveled ecumenical religious music publisher and speaker. My spiritual journey as an adult has taken me to a lot of places as well. One of the results is that I have seen nearly every kind of thing that is done nowadays in the name of Christian worship. A few things have escaped me—I have missed out on the snake handlers in Georgia and I have never been to the Vatican—but I have not missed much.

I have been called to worship by praise choruses and gospel tunes, Wesley hymns and Latin chants. I have sung along with rock and roll bands, down-home gospel quartets, cathedral choirs, and string ensembles.

I have entered the courts of praise when they were in dusty circles around a campfire, in tents with sawdust on the floor, in convention centers with big screens provided so that we could see what was going on up on the stage because it was so far away, in candlelit monastery chapels, in cathedrals in which you could hardly breathe for the weight of the history that is present there, and nearly everywhere in between.

I have stood shoulder to shoulder with charismatics, fundamentalists, evangelicals, Jesus freaks, mainstreamers, and all manner of liturgical folks. I have smelled the incense, shaken a tambourine, genuflected before the altar, bowed as the cross is carried past in procession, and passed the peace. I have prayed through, prayed silently, prayed collects, prayed Psalms, and chanted night prayers. I have heard evangelists, preachers, ministers, deans, canons, bishops, superintendents, chaplains, lay ministers, and all other kinds of authorities as they stood in front of some portion of the faithful and sermonized.

I myself have been a special speaker, a keynote addresser, a guest testifier, a retreat leader, and a lay reader. I have taught a Sunday school class, led a church school class, coordinated a Christian adult education hour, and lectured in a symposium.

And now, if by no other authority than the fact that I have seen more than some, I am going to attempt to reveal the secret of true Christian worship.

　　　　　　　　⬚⬚⬚⬚⬚⬚⬚

Like many people, I have studied just enough Church history to be dangerous. I have not studied enough to know all of the ins and outs of how all of these different things that we do in the name of worship got started, but I have studied enough to know where our worship first began and a little of what it was like.

The way that we Christians worship and much of its form, shape, and content has its roots in an ancient letter known as *The First Apology of Justin the Martyr.*

Justin was a teacher in the church at Rome in the second century after Christ. Around A.D. 150, he wrote a letter to a friend to explain what the community did whenever they would gather. The letter survived the centuries and has become one of the points of origin for our worship. Wherever one goes and whatever is done in the name of Christian worship, that worship has its roots in the words of this ancient letter. I still love to read the letter and let my imagination and memory wander through the things that I have seen and heard in the communities where I have worshiped.

On Sunday we all have an assembly at the same place in the cities or the countryside, and the memoirs of the apostles and the writings of the prophets are read as long as time allows. When the reader has finished the president makes an address, an admonition, and an exhortation about the imitation of these good things. Then we all arise together and offer prayers; and . . . when we have finished there is brought up bread and wine and water, and the president offers in like manner prayers and thanksgivings, as much as he is able, and the people cry out saying the Amen.

The distribution and sharing is made to each from the things over which thanks have been said, and is sent to those not present through the deacons. The well-to-do and those who are willing give according to their pleasure, each one of his own as he wishes, and what is collected is handed over to the president, and he helps widows and orphans, and those who are needy because of sickness or for any other reason, and those who are in prison and the strangers on their journeys.

By and large, the pattern that Justin describes is the same pattern we follow today, whether we are aware of it or not. It is true from the Biltmore Holiness Temple to the First So-and-So Church on the corner to the Abbey of Gethsemani to the Winchester Cathedral and everywhere in between.

For centuries, in groups great and small, in places majestic and mundane, we Christians have done the same: We gather together each week; we offer hymns and songs of praise; we read from the scriptures; we listen as one who has been appointed as our leader offers a sermon; we pray together; we bring forth gifts to be shared with all after the thanksgivings have been said; we give money to be used for the work of the Church and the taking care of the poor; a blessing is pronounced, we respond Amen ("so be it"), and we go out the door to try to be the Body of Christ in the world.

We may comprise several denominations now, even dozens I suppose, but we are one Church–it is evidenced by the pattern of our worship, even if it looks different from place to place.

The differences in liturgies, worship styles, and traditions are clear to anyone who has ever worshiped in churches other than the one in which he or she was introduced to the faith. But even so, if one looks closely, there is a clear sense of the common ancient roots of our worship and of the threads that bind us together. One can still read Justin's letter and see a connection to any Sunday morning service, provided that one is willing to look. And if one is, then one can see that we are brothers and sisters to each other, and not really strangers at all.

There it is, or at least there it is to me–the secret of Christian worship. Wherever and whenever we see those things being done, those elemental practices of worship, then we are in the presence of those who are doing their level best to worship in spirit and in truth. If we do not like the style in which others worship, a style that reflects a collective taste and tradition that is not our own, then we may wrestle with those worshipers about form and taste but not theology. Taste is not a grounds for theological certainty or theological nit-picking.

We are welcome to say that *we* do not like what this group does about this or that part of worship, but we need to be very careful about declaring that we know whether or not *God* likes it. It helps to remember that the worship is not for us anyway, it is for God. It behooves us to use caution when we start to tell others just what particular praises God will or will not inhabit. There is scriptural evidence to suggest that God has gone for everything from dancing naked before the Lord to sacrificing lambs to speaking in tongues to blowing a ram's horn to going off to a mountain to pray alone.

I happen to be of the opinion at this point in my life that God would choose Bach over rock and roll, but who am I to say? Who are any of us to say what God loves to hear from those whom God loves?

❧❧❧❧❧❧❧

Before we were married, the woman who patiently shares my life and generously shares hers with me suggested that we find a new place to attend church together. Along with the other things that we have in common—a love for books and baseball and long stretches at the beach and old roses and lazy Saturdays knocking around town with each other— is a love for the liturgy of the Church.

We were both raised as Nazarenes, but some years before we met, she had made a long journey from the Nazarene

Church to the Episcopal Church. For my part, I had moved in the same direction, only I had only gone along as far as the Methodists. I did not realize it at the time, but I attended what may well have been the most Anglican Methodist church in the entire denomination. Each worship service there was formal and liturgical, so much so that one would be hard-pressed to tell the difference between it and the Episcopal church that we now attend. We attended the Methodist church together for a few weeks, and it looked as though we might decide it was our home church, but after a while, we decided to try some other places. "Church shopping" is the phrase that people use, though we did not actually want to buy one; we just wanted to have a place where we both felt comfortable joining our voices with some portion of the future company of heaven. For her, and now for me, taking the Eucharist once a month was not enough. One needed to take it every Sunday, she said, "or else it just doesn't seem like church to me."

I was in Florida not very long ago because I had been asked to lead a retreat for a group from a large independent church. When I arrived, I was told that the church had about nine thousand members and was still growing. It is one of a number of what are known as mega-churches, which have grown up around the country in recent years. One of the characteristics of such churches is that they generally invent their worship as they go along. And I say that in admiration more than anything else.

A new church that is part of an established denomination has a set of forms, habits, and practices for worship that are built into the fabric of the place. These independent churches, however, must constantly wrestle with defining what is worship for their congregation and what is not. It is complicated by the fact that most everyone who attends such churches came from some other place along the pew that makes up the whole Church; most everyone is a former something–former Nazarene, former Catholic, former Methodist, former Baptist, and so on.

Consequently, figuring out what constitutes worship in such a place is tricky work, and one cannot help but admire those who attempt it. In this particular case, the church leadership must be doing something in the neighborhood of right, because nine thousand people do not show up on Sunday simply because someone is a good preacher or a good marketer or a good anything, for that matter. If worship in the truest sense was not taking place there, then people would have stopped coming a long time ago.

During the workshop sessions of the retreat, I was trying to share with them the things that I had learned about the ancient traditions and practices of contemplative Christian prayer. Before and after those sessions, we would gather up to say the liturgy of the hours, the ancient daily liturgical prayer of the Church. Those ancient prayers, with their psalms and collects and silences, with their monastic feel and tone, were unfamiliar to a lot of the people who attended this mega-church. The juxtaposition of the workshops, the saying of the hours, and their regular worship practices made for some interesting conversations.

One afternoon, on the way back from evening prayers, I was strolling along the path up the hill to the building in which we took our meals together. A woman came along and asked if we could talk. She introduced herself to me as a fellow former Nazarene, then she began to tell me about her own journey. The main point of the story seemed to be for her to explain to me why she had left. She finally left, she said, because she had begun to feel as though she could not worship there anymore. She had a very strong sense of having been driven away, and of having been finally freed from the way that those at her former church worshiped. She had come to believe that they clearly did not have it right somehow, and she was glad to have finally gotten away from them to a church where she felt that true worship was taking place. She felt as though she was very fortunate to have escaped to a church where there was a more formal worship.

After dinner, I went for a walk down toward the river, and a man joined me, hoping he could talk to me for a bit. (I am learning that being a retreat leader is largely a matter of strolling along the right path at the right time.) He introduced himself as a former Roman Catholic who had fled the crowd that he grew up with some years before. He had grown weary of the formal worship and the ritual and the liturgy and the proscribed language of the prayers. It could have been my own insecurity, but I sensed that he was trying to warn me about the slippery slope that I was on, perhaps even wanting to save me from the things that he had felt compelled to flee so long ago. He told me that he was glad that he had found a place where true worship was taking place. I wondered if he ever had talked with the woman whom I had talked to earlier about these things. I also wondered if they knew that they were in the same place now but were coming from and maybe even still moving in opposite directions.

One of the best things about leading retreats is that I get to have those kind of conversations, the kind that take place around the edges of the work that we do together as groups. One of the worst things is that I do not always know what to say in return until the time is long past. The right thing usually occurs to me when I am on an airplane and on the way home.

What I wish now that I had said clearly—and I am not even certain that I said it at all then, or if I even had the presence of mind to try—is this: Those people, the ones who first taught us the Story and tried to show us its ways—the Nazarenes or Catholics, and everyone else—may well have done some things that helped us to begin to see that this place was not our place anymore. But whatever they did to "drive" us away may well not have been as important as what was "drawing" us away.

Perhaps we were driven away. It is true that churches are made up of people, and people are made up of contradictions and from time to time, we hurt each other the deepest when we are trying to love each other the most.

But it could be just as true that we were drawn away by the One Who made us. Perhaps we were drawn by some deep longing within us for a place from which we might come to see and to hear and maybe even to know God in some way that we could not see at the time. Perhaps we were being drawn to a place where we could offer praise and worship from some previously undisturbed corner in the depths of our hearts. Perhaps we were led to, not driven to, a place where we could worship in spirit and in truth, reflecting the person who we have become. It does not mean that such worship did not take place in our previous church; it may mean that we have been led to a place where we can finally join in with our whole heart and mind and soul and strength.

Perhaps this move was not a sign of failure on their part or on ours, perhaps it was a sign of grace on God's part.

⟨⟨⟨⟨⟨⟨⟨

A few blocks from the house where I live is a church that I pass by almost every day. It has one of those signs out front on which the message is changed each week or so, offering up some pithy phrase that makes you think or laugh or groan. I always read it.

There are a lot of universities, seminaries, and Bible colleges in our town, and this church is in the midst of the college community. A professor at one of the local seminaries made some comments in some of his books about who Jesus was and is and the attention being paid to him has a lot of people in our town upset. There is a lot of talk these days about who is a true Christian and who is not. The local seminarians and theologians and preachers and media have been going at each other lately, pretty hard and pretty publicly.

These days, the sign on the church has had the same message for a while, longer than it usually keeps a message up. It reads MEET THE REAL JESUS HERE ON SUNDAYS. I think I understand what they are trying to say. I also wonder and worry that they suspect that you cannot meet the real Jesus in the other churches down the street.

I suspect that one can indeed meet the real Jesus in that church. I also suspect that it would be hard for *me* to do that there, not because the real Jesus is not there, and not because I do not want to meet him, but simply because much of what they do there on Sunday in the name of Christian worship would not feel like church to me, so it would be hard for me to fully enter in. That is not my fault or theirs, it is just true. It is not wrong or right, it just is.

I hope that they understand that the real Jesus can be found in the place where I go on Sundays, as well as in all the ones that are in between.

If so, then we all are worshiping in spirit and in truth as best we can. I suspect that we are, all of us, and it makes me want to say, "So be it," and sing another chorus or two. Something by Bach, of course, is what I prefer, but we can make some joyful rock 'n' roll noise if you like. God probably will be happy either way.

4

TABLE MANNERS

As God's dear children, try to live in love as

Christ loved you.

—SAINT PAUL

We do not presume to come to this thy table,

O merciful Lord, trusting in our own righteousness,

but in thy manifold and great mercies.

We are not worthy so much as to gather up

the crumbs under thy Table.

But thou art the same Lord

whose property is to always have mercy.

Grant us therefore, gracious Lord,

so to eat the flesh of thy dear Son Jesus Christ,

and to drink his blood,

that we may evermore dwell in him,

and he in us. Amen.

—THE BOOK OF COMMON PRAYER

TWO OR THREE TIMES A YEAR, we pack ourselves into the car and head off down into the Mississippi Delta to visit my mother-in-law. One visit, we surprised her. It was not meant to be a surprise—we had called her and left a message on her answering machine to let her know that we were coming down for the weekend—but she had decided, unbeknownst to her daughters, that the newfangled answering machine they bought her was too much trouble to mess with, and so she never got the message.

That weekend, at the end of a really fine Saturday afternoon drive with her, she said to me, "Robert, I wish that I had known you were coming. I could have been anticipating this good time all week long."

I think of that day and of her mischievous grin nearly every time that we head that way now. It takes about three and a half to four hours for us to get as far as Memphis, driving into the afternoon sun, weaving our way in and out of the traffic. When we arrive at the outskirts of Memphis, we take a ring road that heads south and then curves back west toward the river, and then we drive south on the expressway that heads for the Gulf of Mexico. We cross the state line into Mississippi and get off the highway at Bullfrog Corner, onto a two-lane road that leads us due west for a few miles, eventually coming through a little draw that is lined with forest on both sides of the road, and then up a little hill.

When we top the hill and start down the other side, toward Highway 61, we are coming to the real Mississippi. We can tell because suddenly the sky is huge, much bigger than it is in Tennessee, or so it seems to me. The valley of the Mississippi River lies in front of us for miles–broad and flat and rich and green and wet–and the sky stretches out the way that it does in places where there are no hills to block the view.

Here in the South, maybe other places, too, people will describe someone by saying that his feet go all the way to the ground. In the Mississippi Delta, the sky goes all the way to the ground and maybe all the way to heaven as well, all the way from Memphis to New Orleans. The first time that I saw it, that wide-open sky, glowing in the twilight, I nearly ran off the road. In most of Tennessee, we do not have a big sky like that, we have too many hills.

Whenever I go to Mississippi, I always look forward to the moment when we drive over the hill and find ourselves looking out into the huge sky. It makes me feel welcomed. Not welcomed home, exactly. I do not live there and never have, but welcome just the same, as though there is plenty of room for even me under that big sky.

We were married in Nashville, where the two of us have lived now for most all of our lives, instead of in Mississippi, where my wife's family is from. We convinced the Mississippi crowd to come north, where most of our friends live. Our wedding was not a large affair by most standards, and it was not covered by the society pages in the local newspapers. But it was good enough that I would have been happy to have attended it even if I had not been the groom.

Whenever I think of our wedding day, I think of what my mother-in-law said years later when we were riding in the car in the Delta sunshine. If I had had any notion that a day as fine as our wedding day was ever going to happen to me, I would have been anticipating it all my life. As it happens, it came and went too quickly, and I wish that I had been more ready. It was a beautiful day, and a beautiful way to spend it.

It was one of the more ecumenical marriage affairs I have ever attended. We said our vows to each other in a little Lutheran church where my grandfather had been the organist for forty years. Other music for the day was provided by a Southern Baptist who was in the process of shoring up his faith with a serious study of the Eastern monastic traditions. (I am pretty certain that he is still the only Zen Baptist I have ever known.)

We used the wedding service from the *1979 Book of Common Prayer of the Episcopal Church,* and it was administered by a dear friend, a woman who was a United Methodist district superintendent at the time. Communion was served by a committee made up of a Nazarene kindergarten teacher, a Methodist lay preacher, a painter who is a Vanderbilt

Divinity School graduate, and an above-average club tennis player whose religious beliefs are deeply held but still somewhat of a mystery even to those who have known him all of his life.

My wife and I served as the ushers for the Communion. It gave us a chance to greet everyone as they left their pew. People would get up and start forward, and we got to hug them and be hugged in return. Everyone in the place had a chance to grin at us and giggle and say something sweet in our ear as they made their way to the Table.

One of the couples that came to our wedding did not get up to greet us along with the rest. The church that they are a part of had taught them that there was something about the Table in a Lutheran church that made it wrong for them to break the Bread and share the cup with us. I can still see them, in my memory, sitting there in their pew, looking lost and lonely. And it makes me feel the same, even now.

⬛⬛⬛⬛⬛⬛

My journey in search of what it means to pray, to learn to pay attention for the voice and the heart and the presence of the One Who made us, has taken me to a lot of places. Not surprisingly, having spent a number of years in the liturgical tradition, I have more than a few priests in my life now.

Some of them are well-known priests that I have met only in books—Thomas Merton, Thomas Keating, and others. Some of them I have met in person, priests whose names are not well known—Tom, Geoffrey, Anne, Kenneth, Gordon. Some of them were not called Father, Protestant ministers who were priests to me even though they did not wear a collar–Russell, JV, Nancy Carol, Bob, Sid, and others.

One of the priests that I have known in my life was Greek Orthodox. He was one of the instructors at the Academy for Spiritual Formation, a program that I attended for two years during the nineties. A community of approximately sixty people met at a retreat center in northern Alabama four times each year for a week at a time in order to learn more about what it means to live a life of prayer. We spent one of those weeks learning from Father John about praying with icons and other aspects of ancient Orthodox Christian prayer from a part of the Church that is largely unknown to our Western Protestant experience. Father John is a person whom one might describe as operating from a deep well.

Each evening at vespers, the community would gather up to say our prayers and to take the Eucharist. The chairs in the room were arranged in a horseshoe shape with the Table at the open end. After the prayers and the sermon, and the opening liturgy of the Communion itself, we would slowly move around in a circle, making our way toward the front of the room, where we would be served the bread and the cup. On some days, we would sing quietly together as we walked; on others, we would be silent while a piano played softly.

However, Father John never left his seat. Each time that we took the Eucharist, he would simply sit there. He would fold his hands in his lap, and look toward the Table from his seat at the opposite end of the circle, and tears would roll down his face. His church would allow him to teach us to pray, but not to share the Eucharist with us.

For some years after my time at the Academy was over, I traveled along on the course of my spiritual journey with two good friends whom I met there. We lived in three different states and would see each other two or three times each year for retreat. In between, we stayed in touch by telephone and by mail, and by virtue of a common rule for prayer and accountability that we had adopted.

Most often when the three of us went on retreat together, we used a pattern for the day of reading and contemplation, of study and prayer that we had adopted from the daily rule of the Academy. A few times, we arranged to spend our retreat with yet another priest we had met at the Academy. Father Ed had become a kind of spiritual father for all three of us.

We met with him in Florida once, sharing a house beside a lake. There were the three of us and Father Ed and a friend of his from Michigan. Father Ed led us through a series of reflective exercises each day, and in the evenings we would help each other prepare and serve a meal and then we would go for walks or read or talk. At about five o'clock each day, he would break my heart.

Part of our practice whenever the three of us were on retreat was to take the Eucharist together each day. Part of his practice was to take it each evening as his workday ended. So we all gathered up around the dining room table together.

The priest and his friend would be at one end of the table, my two Methodist friends at the other end. I, as the resident Episcopalian, was in the middle, of course.

Father Ed would pass around the Catholic service books that he had brought, and we would read through the service together, offer our prayers together, read the scriptures, and join our voices with angels and archangels and all the company of heaven.

Then came the moment when he would begin to prepare the bread and the wine, saying the prayers and making the signs and gestures of the ritual. At the other end of the table, my friend the Methodist minister would do the same thing to another loaf of bread and to another cup of wine. Father Ed could pray with us, teach us, walk beside us, encourage us, and say the liturgy with us, but he could not break the bread and share the cup with us. And it just broke my heart back then, and it still does. And his as well, I believe.

Years later, as I sat in the sixth row on a Christmas morning at a little church in the Delta, my heart began to go from broken to angry. I do not like to admit that, but I am afraid that it is true.

※※※※※

For many years now, I have gone to church on Christmas Eve for the midnight service that celebrates the coming of the Light of the world, the Light that will enlighten us all. I like it best when we do not travel, and I am able to be at the cathedral parish at which we are members. It is home to me. But if we are traveling for Christmas, it is always to the Delta, and there is an Episcopal church a few blocks from my mother-in-law's house, so we attend their midnight service. It is not home, but it is close.

One year, we were late getting away from the city to get to the Delta for the holiday. We missed the big sky moment as we came over the hill outside Memphis because it was already dark by the time we turned south, and we missed the Christmas Eve service at the little Episcopal church because it was already over by the time that we arrived.

So I set my alarm for early in the morning, figuring that I would go to the Christmas Day service, only to discover when I called to see what time it started that there was no Christmas morning service at the Episcopal church. The priest served two parishes, and on Christmas he had to be at the other one, an hour's drive away. I made some other calls and discovered that the rest of the Protestants were home with Santa Claus. For those of us who were inclined to go to church on Christmas in this particular small town in Mississippi, there was only one place to be.

I arrived at the local Catholic church early, knowing that the order of service and the books to use would be a little different from what I was used to, and I wanted to have plenty of time to get organized so that I would not be lost the whole time. I do not like to look like a tourist even in small towns where no one knows me. There was probably no way that anyone in the room knew that I had only recently been confirmed in the Episcopal Church, but I did not want to let the Canterbury side down by looking lost in the liturgy in front of a crowd of Catholics.

By the time that everyone else arrived, though, I was ready. In the quiet that you find in churches as people gather, I had had a few moments alone to consider the great question–the question that had kept me from going to a Catholic church for years.

The great question for many of us whenever we worship with our brothers and sisters in a Catholic church has to do with whether or not we are going to take the Eucharist. We know enough to know that we are really not supposed to. As a rule, we are willing to be gracious guests, respect the tradition and practice of the place in which we are worshiping, and simply sit in our pews while the chosen ones go forward to the Table.

The truth is that all churches have customs and practices that may cause consternation to those who visit, so I suppose that it evens out. We all try our best to honor the traditions and the teachings of those who have gone before us, and rightly so. In the spirit of Christmas, I had prepared myself to behave myself.

At first, I thought that I would just do the expected thing: go to the altar, cross my arms over my chest, and receive a blessing. The priest would assume that I was a Catholic who did not happen to be in a state of grace, but I figured I could live with that. No matter what state that I am in, I ordinarily receive more grace in a given day than I deserve anyway. And then I thought that maybe I would just sit in my seat quietly and leave it at that. While I sat pondering the question, I read the paragraph on the back of the bulletin that had to do with who should come to the Table and who should not.

The paragraph started out by saying that I was welcome to come to worship, pray the prayers, sing the songs, and put money in the offering plate for the poor. It went on to say that they were glad to have me there and hoped I would come back. And then the paragraph noted that they would love to serve me the Eucharist, but that to do so "implies a unity in the Church that does not yet exist."

I understand that. I only had to remember the nobility and the anguish, the honor and the struggle of Father John and Father Ed to know that some of the people in the room with me on that Christmas morning were likely in some amount of consternation about the need for the paragraph as well.

Even so, I thought to myself, the truth is that to *not* serve us all reinforces the notion of a disunity that is at odds with the Sacrifice itself. It also occurred to me that unity in the Body of Christ was going to be hard to ever come by if we kept figuring out ways to keep the Light of the world in a box marked "for members of our group only."

I thought about the first Table, the one that our Lord set with his own two hands, the one that was open to Judas, who later betrayed him, and Peter, who later denied him, and Thomas, who later doubted him, and the ones who could not stay awake to pray with him. I wondered what that implied.

It was hard to sit still and be a gracious guest, but I did

my best to emulate Father John. I sat there thinking of skies that were big enough for even me and praying for Tables at which all God's children would be welcome.

My two Academy friends and I went to Cincinnati for a weeklong workshop that was being held in a place that had once been a convent. The workshop was to begin on Monday morning, but I drove in early on Sunday afternoon in order to have a chance to settle in, get comfortable, and wander the grounds, halls, and buildings a bit.

It is always moving for me to walk around such a place, a place where people have given their entire lives over to God. I am always touched by the plain and simple furnishings, the small rooms that were once the cells of the nuns, the quiet courtyards between the buildings. There is inevitably a sense of peace and solitude in such a place, even when it is found in the midst of a city.

I do not know all the history of this particular place, but evidently a portion of the community there had been cloistered. The other part of the community was made up of nuns who were teachers at the school that was a couple blocks up the street.

There was also a parish church on the convent grounds, and the sanctuary was divided into two parts. About three-quarters of it was used for the public worship that was held there; the setup looked like any other church, with pews and aisles that led to the altar. But behind the altar was another space, a space for the cloistered nuns to worship with the congregation, in the presence of the altar but out of sight of the public. The Table was on a raised platform, with a cross suspended from the ceiling over it. The altar's placement sort of turned the church into two rooms. You could see the altar from either of the "rooms," but you could not see into the other room.

On that Sunday afternoon, I wandered my way around until I found a doorway into the little cloister chapel behind the altar. It was okay for me to be there now because some years before, the community had dispersed and the complex had been purchased by a group of laypeople, who had converted it into an ecumenical retreat center. Retreatants were assigned to stay in the cells that used to be the home of the nuns, so I figured that the chapel behind the altar was a place that I could go as well.

The nuns had left, but their presence had not. It lingered in the chapel's room, or so it seemed to me. I sat there in the cool and the silence for most of the afternoon. Later, when my two friends arrived, I told them that I had found just the place for us to say our prayers each day, as was our custom whenever we were together.

The next afternoon, at the end of the workday, so to speak, we three Protestants went off to say our prayers and to take the Eucharist. The dozen or so Catholics who were also attending the workshop went off to do the same.

We were a little more than halfway through the liturgy, at the part at which the Prayer of Humble Access is said, when I began to hear murmuring voices from somewhere. "We do not presume to come to this thy Table, O merciful Lord, trusting in our own righteousness," we were saying.

"We are not worthy so much as to gather up the crumbs under thy Table."

I thought to myself that I sure wished whoever was outside in the hallway would not presume to talk so loudly while others were taking the Eucharist. The voices were not so loud that I could hear what the speakers were saying, but they were loud enough to be distracting. As the murmurings began to become annoying, I found it harder and harder to be as pious and reverent as I felt that I ought to be. Here I was being holy, and some noisy crowd was in the hallway catching up on the news.

In the liturgical practice of the Eucharist, there is a moment in which someone or everyone together offers an Alleluia. The ritual varies from place to place, and in some places the congregation will sing a chorus of a song as the bread and the wine and the Table are being prepared.

It turned out that the murmuring was actually the sound of the Catholics in the church on the other side of the altar. At about the same time that they began to sing their Alleluia, we were just about ready to sing ours over on our side. My friends and I looked at one another and just grinned, and the murmuring went from annoying to holy. Then the singer in our group—the other two of us are not really singers at all—recognized the Catholics' tune and began to sing the same song in a kind of round or response with the people on the other side of the altar.

To be sure, it was a sweet moment for us all, even though we could not see one another. It was a moment in which one could believe that what binds us together and what we hold in common is more powerful than what keeps us apart.

The overlapping of Alleluias only happened the one day that week. After that, both groups, probably to keep from disturbing each other, did not sing their Alleluias anymore. Instead, each spoke them quietly and kept them to themselves. Perhaps had we done it all week, the walls between us might have begun to come tumbling down. Such a thing happened in Jericho once; it might have happened in Cincinnati if we had tried.

※※※※※※

I have been told that Brother Roger, the legendary founder of the ecumenical community at Taize in France, serves the Eucharist each day to those who gather there. But each day, he himself does not partake. He is waiting, he says, for the time when we can all partake together.

"This is not the Table of this congregation, nor is it the Table of this denomination, it is the Table of the Lord. And it is, therefore, a Table to which everyone present is invited." I have a friend who says that every Sunday to his congregation when he has finished the rituals and the rubrics that are performed to prepare the Table.

The actions of both men are acts of courage—the self-sacrifice of the one who chooses to serve and not partake, and the openhearted generosity of the one who serves everyone who comes. Both positions are consistent with the Gospel. The third position, the one that says this Christian can come to the table but that one cannot, is very hard to square with the Gospel.

The Table does not belong to us, to any one group, no

matter who we are. It belongs to all of us. The gifts of God for the people of God are just that–gifts. To withhold them from the others who are called by his name is to denigrate the Sacrifice itself.

⸎⸎⸎⸎⸎⸎

Each morning, when I am up early enough to be in my studio before the traffic begins to make too much rush hour noise, I can hear the bells ring at a church a few blocks from my house. Each morning, those bells call out to say that the Body is being broken and the Blood is being shared–come and dine. Each morning, my heart calls to me to walk those few blocks and to break bread with my brothers and sisters. Each morning, the worshipers at that church do not presume to go to the Table trusting in their own righteousness, but they are told they must presume that I should not join them. According to someone in authority somewhere– someone who cares, someone who honestly and fervently seeks to honor their tradition, perhaps even someone who has Father John's tears in his eyes–to welcome me to the Table implies a unity that is not yet a reality, even though it is a reality to me and to most of those who gather up each morning at the ringing of those bells.

My heart has been broken at the Table where the bread is broken in Jacksonville and Mississippi and Cincinnati and Nashville and a lot of other places beyond and in between. It has been broken on retreats and on holy days and on my wedding day, and it will be broken again tomorrow when I hear those bells ringing across my neighborhood.

I do not believe that I am alone. Our hearts are broken because we are somehow capable—day after day, week after week, knowingly or unknowingly—of using the great common denominator of our faith to divide ourselves from each other.

This dividing is surely not the reason why the Body of Jesus was broken in the first place, but it may well be among the reasons why the whole Body of Christ is difficult to find in our world. We who claim it sometimes cannot even share it with each other.

A better day is coming, a day with a big sky, where there is room for everyone to stand in the sunlight. And there will be a Table to which everyone is invited, just like the first one.

I am not sure when we will get there, but I have been anticipating just such a good time all week.

5

THE STUDENT BODY OF CHRIST

You must work out your own salvation in fear and trembling;

for it is God who works in you, inspiring both the will and

the deed, for his own chosen purpose.

—SAINT PAUL

Almighty God, thou hast built thy Church

upon the foundations of the apostles and the prophets,

Jesus Christ himself being the chief cornerstone:

Grant us so to be joined together in unity of spirit

by their teaching,

that we may be made a holy temple acceptable to thee.

And grant us the gift of thy Holy Spirit,

that we may be devoted to thee with our whole heart,

and united to one another in pure affection;

through Jesus Christ our Lord, who lives and reigns

with thee and the Holy Spirit. Amen.

—*THE BOOK OF COMMON PRAYER*

I LIVE IN A TOWN where people love the Bible. In fact, some of the locals refer to it as "the buckle of the Bible Belt." Everyone, or so it seems sometimes, is on their way to or from a Bible study. I have ended up in a lot of conversations about what the Bible means and where it comes from, and how we are to go about wrestling with it.

In some conversations, I find people who believe that the books of the Bible were dictated by God. They believe that those words are to be taken literally, and that there are no inconsistencies in them and no contradictions, either. The scriptures and the study of them are at the center of their Christian faith.

A different opinion is had by people who believe that although the Bible is divinely inspired, it also must be understood as the work of men and women who were human. This means that the words themselves have to be constantly wrestled with in the light of scholarship, tradition, and the times in which we live.

Both sides are full of well-intentioned, faithful, thought-ful, compassionate, and devout people. Both sides have scholars to whom they look for knowledge, preachers to whom they look for instruction, and commentators to whom they look for guidance. Both sides are capable of forbear-ance, wisdom, and compassion; both sides are guilty of in-tolerance, close-mindedness, and intimidation.

It is true that the orthodox, be they liberal or conserva-tive, mainline or evangelical, by and large get nervous if you even look like you are questioning their view of the way that the canon of the scriptures is to be regarded. Some of them are worried that you are trying to water the scriptures down. Others are worried that you are putting your head in the sand.

Then there are the rest of us, people who are not schol-ars, theologians, apologists, or commentators. We are simply people in the pews who are trying to learn to be faithful and trying to learn to listen for the voice of God.

And some of us are really afraid of the conversations. Some of us are afraid that we will get it wrong and will not be in that number when the saints go marching in. Others of us are afraid of being on the wrong side and being guilty by association. Still others are afraid that someone will find out that we are not completely certain about the things that we are supposed to be so certain about.

I am not afraid of the conversations, though I try to tread lightly. I have friends who are pretty well dug in on both sides of the line, and I like having my friends, so I have learned to be careful. I am afraid that I am going to be walking down the street one day, someone is going to recognize me, and my children will not be allowed to attend church camp anymore.

I read some of the the books that are published in defense of one side of the conversation or the other. And I engage in the talk and follow the arguments on both sides. I read the debunkers and their debunkers, too. Then I grin and remember that we are all pilgrims on a journey of faith, not certainty.

And although I have loved reading all the books, admire the people who write them, and consider their contribution to the general discussion to be valuable, I have to say that some of the arguing that goes on in them has meant that I and a lot of others have spent a fair amount of time talking and wrestling over things that we will never know while we are here on this earth. We may know them in the kingdom that is yet to come, but here and now, while we are living in the kingdom that has already come, we are going to have to live with some holes in our knowledge.

Sometimes when I am listening, literally or figuratively, to the two sides argue back and forth, it reminds me of when the cover of *Time* magazine asked the question, "Is God Dead?" All manner of dire predictions were made about what would happen if such stories continued to be written and people started to read them. One thing that clearly happened was that it caused a large number of us to look deeply inside ourselves and finally respond, "No, I do not believe God is dead," with more clarity and conviction than we had in some time, even though we were no more able to prove that God exists than we could before. The media stories, sermons, soul-searching, and discussions did not kill God any more than they might have invented him. And to be fair, the asking of the question and the attempt to try to answer it honestly probably did not do God's friends any harm at all in the long run.

So the back-and-forth conversations do not make me nervous. I do not think we are going to put the scriptures out of business. I am hoping that the continuing conversation will lead us closer and closer to what I think is the point: How are we supposed to live with each other?

❦❦❦❦❦❦

I came across a translation of the New Testament once in which the word *disciple* is translated as "student." Jesus was the Teacher; the ones who listened to him and then chose to follow him were his students. He came to teach them about the kingdom that had already come and that was to come even still, somehow. They came to him to learn how to recognize it as well as to live in and out of it. If they would listen to his teaching, he would teach them how to live in the way that God had envisioned for them all.

Of all of the names that we have for the Son of God—Christ, Master, Lord, Redeemer, Messiah, Savior—one that often gets the least attention is Teacher. Not, perhaps, because it is the most esoteric, abstract, or difficult to understand, but perhaps precisely because it is the easiest to understand. It is the one that is the closest to us and our experience, the one that is the closest to our status here on earth. We know something about teachers and students, and we have been one or the other or even both in our lives. However, we do not have much experience being Messiahs.

I do not always know exactly how I am to live in relationship to the Messiah. I was not really looking for one when this one found me. But now that I have been found, I might do well to listen to the Teacher. I am in need of someone who can teach me the ways of God, the ways to live so that I might become a reasonable facsimile of the person who I am supposed to become, the ways to become a reasonable and lively version of the saint who I was envisioned to become when God dreamed me into being in the first place.

But most of us seldom think of ourselves as the students of the Teacher. We are Christians: card-carrying members of institutions that have codified his teaching after all these years. In the name of becoming the mature Christians that Saint Paul envisioned, we too often forsake becoming and remaining the hungry students whom Jesus sought out and called his own.

Jim Wallis once wrote that many of us "skip the prophets, go straight to John 3:16, and then on to Saint Paul." We do not miss a great deal, of course, just the teachings of the One Who came among us to teach us how to live with each other. In our haste to clearly define what it means to be "the true Body of Christ," we often miss the continuing call to be "the student Body of Christ." We often behave as though we have nothing more to learn about those things.

We have a Teacher, one who came into our midst to teach us the way to live, but we spend a fair amount of our

time, especially our time spent parsing the scriptures into little bits and pieces, straining at gnats and swallowing camels.

✦✦✦✦✦

I generally believe that we who call ourselves Christians are
pretty good folks. I also happen to think that we would be
even better folks if we actually believed the Gospel.

Oh, we like to sing about it, quote it, argue about it, pub-
lish it, spread it around, and pack it under our arms on Sunday mornings, but it is by no means completely clear that
we take it completely seriously, or at least not as seriously as
we ought to, or even as seriously as we claim to.

I am not willing to go so far as to use the term *hypocrites,*
if for no other reason than that I am included in that number. I, too, hope to be one of the saints marching in or
marching out or wherever it is that we are all going. Maybe
the term that I am looking for is *hard of hearing.* Or hardly
hearing at all.

✦✦✦✦✦

One can make a case that we Christians have not always understood the scriptures, anyway. In fact, it is only in the past
few hundred years that the scriptures were in languages that
most of us could read, and it was not too long ago, histori-
cally speaking, that most of the people on the planet could
not read.

In our best moments down across the years, we Christians

have been known to use the scriptures as motivation for the building of hospitals and schools, the teaching of farming and medicine to people, the comforting of the afflicted, and the marching for justice and peace, all for the sake of the kingdom. But we are also the ones who read the scriptures and then instituted the Inquisition, propped up slavery in our own pulpits, defended the Vietnam war for the sake of national pride, and quietly wished that Martin Luther King Jr. and his friends would quiet down.

Have you ever said to yourself that if you had been alive when Jesus was around that you would not have been as foolish as the rich young ruler? It is so easy for us to talk about his greed and not talk about the way that some of us who can afford summer homes are not willing for the government to spend money for houses for people who live under park benches.

How can the religious establishment of Jesus' day not have understood something so simple and clear as "Love your enemy"? we say to ourselves—as we ignore the embargo on the people in Cuba, the one that we keep in place for the sake of "bringing down an enemy" who cannot even hurt us.

How can the Jews not have seen that Jesus came for the Gentiles, too? we say—as we vote for the people who promise to keep the immigrants away.

It has always been easier to talk about how Jesus said what he said and where he said it than it has been to listen to what he said to those who would follow him. It is easier to talk about the accuracy of the scriptures than it is about what it will take for us to enter the kingdom. It is always easier to wrestle over manuscripts and origins and time frames and translations than it is to wrestle with how we are supposed to live.

"The trouble with really seeing and really hearing," wrote Frederick Beuchner, "is that then we really have to do something about what we have seen and heard." What God had to say to those who heard him first—and what he has to say to us today—is a good deal clearer, more simple, and more direct than we would like for it to be.

And when the words of the Teacher become too clear, it makes us uncomfortable, because then we have to choose between living out the lesson or clouding it over. Anyone who is trying to save his life rather than lose it knows that confusion can be a pretty good defense. At least, in the short term.

❧❧❧❧❧

It is an honest and, in many ways, perfectly reasonable reaction for us to sometimes want to ignore the words of Jesus. Most of the time, his words are not perfectly reasonable at all.

In a liturgy that is used in the place where I worship, the priest will sometimes say, "Hear these comfortable words of Jesus," and I always sort of brace myself. I am waiting for the day when she says, "Hear these disturbing, terrifying, unsettling, and astonishing words of Jesus." For that is what many of his words are. Who can blame us for wanting to argue about the scriptures rather than listen to them?

For what Jesus had to say to those who would follow him, to his students, suggests a way to live that is very unlike the way that many of us live our lives. His reassurance that we will make a contribution to a kingdom that we may or may not ever see or recognize in our lifetime is hardly reassuring enough to change our lives for. If we become really good at living the life of Jesus, we can lose our status, our possessions, and our retirement plan, and get murdered by a crowd of religious folks. No wonder nobody wants to listen to him.

"I think everybody wants to go to heaven," my father used to say, "but if I announce that there is a train leaving for heaven in twenty minutes, the line will not be very long." And if you think *that* line is short, try the one marked "Lay down your life" or "Sell all you have and give it to the poor" or "Give to everyone who begs of you" or "Do good to those who hate you."

We cannot have it both ways: We cannot say that we want to go to heaven when we die, and then live as though we are afraid to die. We cannot claim to follow the Christ, yet ignore the Teacher. We cannot call ourselves his disciples, yet fail to be his students. "A house divided will fall," the Teacher said, and what he said is true. Arguing about the size of the house or the definition of *fall* does not change the truth of what Jesus said.

Sometimes, people who did not grow up under the influences that many of us did can see that the more they come to know about Jesus, the less that we longtime worshipers look like the followers of Jesus, and the more we look like the foolish brood of Jerusalem.

Maybe, I think to myself, if we could allow the words of the Teacher to live and take root in us, to grow in us more freely, we might become bearers of the kingdom rather than merely a crowd who is squabbling over who is right and who is more right while we all become more lost.

We who claim his name and believe in him must learn to stop wrestling over the details about the scriptures and learn to follow him. We must learn to live as though he is among us still. We need to know that he still speaks our name from time to time as simply and clearly as he did to the fishermen, tax collectors, prostitutes, and others who asked where he was going and if they could come along.

If we are to follow him, we must listen to him. We must become his students again, or even for the first time. We must listen to what he said to those who followed him. No matter how divinely or haphazardly it was recorded, no matter how it has been used for ill or for good in the past, no matter how difficult it is to hear him above the clatter and clamor of our world and our Church and our own troubled hearts.

For those of us who would follow, there is only one question: What did Jesus say to those who said that they wanted to go with him? And how do we hide those things in our hearts until we become true students of the Teacher, faithful disciples of the Master, recognizable followers of the Christ, fellow heirs of the kingdom?

I am neither a scholar nor a theologian. I am little more than a pilgrim who is trying to love God with all my mind, all my heart, and all my soul. And I am reasonably certain that I am not alone in that. I am just trying to follow him based on the voice of the Teacher and what that voice says to me, in the stories in the Gospels and in the silence of my heart and in the way that it speaks to me in my life.

Even if I knew all of the answers to all of the questions over which all of these arguments rage, what would I have found that would change what I am to do next?—which is to listen and learn and try to live his teachings.

My struggle is not with whether or not the scriptures that have been given to us are real or whether or not they contain the truth. My struggle is not with whether or not I think God is who I think he is, it is with what I believe that he is saying to me and to us all; it is with what to do with and about those teachings as I try to live a life that can be called the life of a disciple, a student, if you will. And I think that I am not alone in that, either.

I am well aware that there are those among us for whom discussions and questions about the history of the scriptures are very important. I do not mean to suggest that I have wrestled all of those questions to the ground for myself or anyone else. For all I know, I am simply weary or lazy, or something even worse, rather than at peace about them.

I am simply saying that for me, at this point in my life, and for many of us, I believe, a lot of those questions are ones that we may well never know the answers to and are no longer the ones that ring in my heart or trouble my soul—

even if this fact means that I have to live with an awful lot of unanswered questions.

"Life is not a problem to be solved," wrote Thomas Merton, "it is a mystery to be lived." I believe there is a good chance that is especially true, and gloriously so, of a life lived under the influence of the scriptures.

I believe that Jesus is the Son of God, that he lived then and that he lives now, that he called others before us to follow him and that he calls us yet today. These are mysteries that I cannot explain to you or myself or anyone else to the complete satisfaction of us all. But even so, what I want to do now more than anything else is to stand shoulder to shoulder with others who share that faith, and to learn more and more about what it means to live a life based on Jesus' teachings.

I am still listening for the same thing that I have been listening for since I was old enough to sit in a church pew: What did the Teacher say to those who were his students, those who said they wanted to follow him?

<hr/>

I talk about all these things with people that I meet. When my wife hears me discussing such things with our friends, she asks them to pray for her. She is afraid that she is sleeping with a heretic she tells them, and I think she is kidding.

What often happens when I am having a conversation about the scriptures with someone is that for one reason or another—fear of something, perhaps, on both sides—we end up saying to each other, "Well, it is obvious that we disagree," and we smile and say things about being brothers anyway.

But I am afraid that sometimes under our breath we are saying, "So I will question your authenticity as a Christian, and you can make a judgment about mine. I will hold this position, and you hold that one; you stay on your side, and I will stay on mine. You go off and live as though you have a corner on the truth, and I will assume that I do."

One of us, God knows, may be right. Or neither of us, for that matter. No one can say for certain. But what I can say is this: Such posturing does more to destroy the kingdom than it does to build it.

We are not called to be right; we are called to be his. We are not called to be scholars; we are called to be students. We are not called to explain the Christ; we are called to follow the Christ. We are not called to build walls that keep his friends apart from each other; we are called to build the kingdom together.

It may turn out to be easier to get through the eye of a needle, one might say, but it is a journey that we must attempt. The kingdom is on the other side.

6

PASSING THE PIECE

Why do you hold your brother in contempt?

We shall all stand before God.

Each of us will have to answer for ourselves.

—SAINT PAUL

Almighty God, who by thy Holy Spirit,

hast made us one with thy saints in heaven and on earth:

Grant that in our earthly pilgrimage we may ever

be supported by this fellowship of love and prayer,

and may know ourselves to be surrounded by their witness

to thy power and mercy.

We ask this for the sake of Jesus Christ, in whom

all our intercessions are acceptable through the Spirit,

and who liveth and reigneth for ever and ever. Amen.

—THE BOOK OF COMMON PRAYER

ONE TIME WHEN I WAS at a conference as a speaker, a woman sat down next to me at my table at lunch. I say it was *my* table because it was my table; it had a placard in the middle of it that had my name on it.

It is customary at this particular conference to give each speaker a table at meals so that people who want to talk more about the things that they have heard can sit at the speaker's table and have a chance to do just that.

Some of the things that I had been talking about in my sessions had suggested to this woman that I might know about a particular writer whose work she had been reading lately. She was worried about whether or not it was okay to read his books. She was worried that because he was Catholic and she was not, she was in danger of being led astray by the things that he had to say. She was worried because some of her friends and some of the people whom she looked to for guidance in her Christian journey had warned her to stay away from people like him.

I did not tell her that the author she was talking about

was the same man who had played a critical role in my own journey. I did tell her that she need not worry too much; the man was not likely to cause her to fall from grace.

I also did not let on that the whole conversation made me sad. Such fears are often what keep the Body of Christ broken into parts.

Within a couple months after my first book was published, two letters came to my house on the same day.

One was from an old friend of mine, and so I opened it quickly. She was writing to let me know that she was attending a conference, and the man who was to be leading the devotions each morning had told everyone there that he had set aside what he had prepared and was going to read aloud from my book instead.

I knew this man by virtue of his work and had admired him for a long time, though I had never met him. He worships and works in a part of the Church that I do not, and I have to confess that it tickled me to know that he had even read my book. The whole thing just made me grin and feel that something I was doing was beginning to have some meaning beyond the four walls in which I do my writing.

Inside the other envelope was a copy of a review of my book from a major trade magazine that is read by the people who decide whether or not certain books, including mine, are going to end up on certain bookstore shelves. The review advised the people who own Christian bookstores that "if they wanted to be sure that their store remained on firm theological ground," they would be wise not to stock my book.

I came to a couple of conclusions that morning. One is that I should never read a review that someone who loves me has not read first. I am far too thin-skinned to take such chances. I knew better anyway, but I think my excitement about my friend's letter just dazed me for a minute into thinking that I was about to be universally loved and accepted by the whole Church. The review upset me then and it still upsets me.

A few days later, I had lunch with a friend, and I told him the story and asked him what he thought. I was worried that maybe I was out there in the dark a little too far, theologically speaking. He assured me that what I had written was clearly within the bounds of orthodoxy, and he is a scholar who should know, and he is a friend who would tell me the truth. It made me feel somewhat better.

Then, with a twinkle in his eye, he added, "But you know, Robert, there are some people who insist on coloring outside the lines. And you may be one of them." I took it as a compliment, but I have always been a little afraid to ask if he meant it as such.

The other thing that struck me the morning I received the letters and that has stayed with me all these years is how sad it is that someone would go out of his way to make sure that people in one part of the Church do not run into the ideas of people from another part, as though such a thing happening would be bad for rather than good for the Church.

In the fall of the year that my father passed away, I went to see some friends of his and of mine at PraiseGathering in Indianapolis. There are usually about ten thousand people there, and the days are filled with workshops and seminars; the evenings are filled with concerts and worship services. It was a homecoming of sorts for me because I used to help behind the scenes at the conference when I was younger. I had not attended in several years.

I fell into my usual habit whenever I am attending large gatherings: that of cruising the conference areas, slipping in and out of side doors and such, listening to a few minutes of everybody's stuff just to see what different speakers are up to. My theory, for better or for worse, and I am certain that it is the latter, is that I can get a pretty good idea as to what people are doing if I cruise the place for about an hour. Then, instead of spending three days sitting in conference rooms and on folding chairs, I could do what I really liked to do at conferences, which is to stay in a nice hotel, eat someone else's cooking, take very long walks interspersed with long naps, and wander my way into animated conversations with the friends that I had come to see. When I am not busy coloring outside the lines, I am usually hanging around the edges.

My "hang around the edges but do not get sucked into an actual workshop plan" was working pretty well until I wandered into the back of a room and heard a little man who referred to himself as a recovering Roman Catholic priest. It was a better than average turn of phrase, so I stopped to listen. I at least wanted to know what he was recovering from, whether it was the Roman part or the Catholic part or something else.

He was telling a story about a priest who had gone back to Ireland to visit a favorite old uncle on the occasion of the old uncle's seventieth birthday. The priest was there for a few days before the old man would even speak to him, and the priest was more than a little annoyed with the old man. Early on the morning of his birthday itself, before the sun was even up, the old uncle awakened the young priest and told him to get dressed; they were going for a walk. They walked for some time in silence, in the gray light of that time of day, until they reached a cliff overlooking the sea. The sun was just coming up out of the sea, all red and pink and on fire. "You see," said the old man, "the Father loves me very, very much."

I do not know why the man who was telling the story that morning in Indianapolis drew me to him so. He was shouting for one thing—okay, preaching some would call it—and I am not normally drawn to such loud oration, but I kept not being able to move. Before it was over, I was pretty much nailed to the back wall, watching huge portions of my life passing before me. I was thinking of my own father, and of how he had spent much of his life trying to teach me the same thing—that the Father, the One Who made us, loves me very, very much—and I was thinking that I believed it more in that moment than I ever had before. I was suddenly wishing that I could tell my father that I finally understood what he had been saying to me all along.

At the end, I quickly slipped out of the room to avoid the crowd. Because I knew the back hallways in the convention center from being there in my younger days, I knew where to find a place to hide from the ten thousand people in the building, and so I did just that—for some hours, actually. I spent the time listening to a conversation that began in my head and in my heart and in my soul that day, and that has continued unabated all these years.

Aunt Bertha, my Nazarene Sunday school teacher, would have said that I was under conviction. My Methodist friends would have quoted John Wesley to me and suggested that my heart had been strangely warmed. My Anglican friends would have termed it a conversion experience. I called it terrifying, and still do.

In my life, I have had maybe one or two such moments when I felt as though God was speaking to me in a very direct and clear way. It is something that I did not completely understand when it happened, and in some ways I understand even less now that I have read a lot of books and know the fancy words and terms for it. What happened was that somewhere, deep inside of me, I heard a voice say something to me. Years later, I can still remember that voice and what the voice said to me. I have never recovered.

I will not tell you what the voice said to me. If anything in my life was ever private, this is it. But I will say this much: What I heard that day is the reason that I have done everything that I have done, both in the name of trying to learn to pray in these past fifteen years or so, and in the name of trying to be an artist. It is the reason that I go to my studio each day and pick up my fountain pen. Whatever term that you want to use for it, it was one of *those* moments.

"What is it that's taken hold of me," wrote Claude Monet to a friend, "for me to carry on like this in relentless pursuit of something beyond my powers?" He could not or would not say a name for what had taken hold of him, either, any more than any of us who have been taken hold of are able to most of the time.

Later, at the Indianapolis gathering, I thought that I might go and tell the man who had been preaching how much his story had meant to me. I was going to tell him that the story of his uncle and his trip to Ireland and what his uncle said to him had somehow shown me the truth of the Gospel in a way that I had never before understood. I was going to tell him that, as strange as it may have seemed to me, I thought I had only just begun to hear the word that God loves me. I felt he would like to hear such a testimonial, and I was certain that I wanted to say it.

But when I found him, I discovered that I could not speak, I could only stand there looking at him. He was about two feet from me and said hello, waiting for me to speak; I was trying to, but no sound would come out, literally.

Finally he spoke. "It is okay, Robert," he said—God only knows how he knew my name because I am not much bigger on name badges than I am on sitting through workshops—"you do not have to say anything, it is written on your face."

So I went back to my hotel across the street and took a look, but I did not see much. I stayed in my room for much of the next two days, then the conference was over, he was gone, and I never really was able to tell him what his story had meant to me.

꧁꧂꧁꧂꧁꧂

It is quite possible that the only organized set of classes or instruction that I ever really attended with any faithfulness in my adult life were the ones at the Academy for Spiritual Formation.

One of the teachers who was there during the last week of the program was a Catholic priest from Detroit. Father Ed is a prototypical urban Irish Catholic priest, like the kind you see in old movies. He is short and round, with a great white beard, a gentle spirit, a rolling lilt to his voice, and eyes that sparkle behind the big black horn-rimmed glasses that he wears. He teaches at a seminary, but he spends much of the year on the road, primarily leading retreats and workshops.

In the course of the week that I first met him, he adopted me, or maybe it was the other way around. At any rate, he became a kind of long-term spiritual companion and guide to me and my two close friends from the Academy. The three of us would make retreats together three or four times a year; for several years, we would figure out a way to spend at least one of those times each year with Father Ed.

In the world of contemplative prayer, the world in which Father Ed was instructing us—not that we were going to become monks, but we hoped to glean something of the life of prayer from those who lived a life of a prayer—there is a practice that I describe as "*getting a word.*" I am certain that it must have a fancier name, I just do not know what it is.

What I mean by this practice is that whenever I make a retreat with Father Ed, I go in search, in a way, of a word of guidance from him to aid me in where I am on my journey at the time. At some point during the retreat, I spend some time with Father Ed, attempting to explain where I think I am in my journey. He listens for a while, asks a question or two, then says a little of what he is hearing in my story and suggests a way that I might adjust my spiritual practice in the next stage of my journey. At times, that moment in the retreat is terribly emotional or difficult; other times, it is quiet and gentle—it always really matters.

Whenever my two Academy friends and I are with Father Ed, the custom is that each of us has our individual moment with Father Ed during one of the afternoons, just after evening prayers but before dinnertime. That is the time of day when he takes his afternoon walk for his health. One of us walks along with him, tells our story, asks our questions, and listens for our word.

We were in Florida and it was hot and muggy, and Father Ed and I were walking along together in the late afternoon. It was his time to listen to me, and it was my time to listen for a word. A few days before, I had received a letter from the man I had heard speak in Indianapolis, the first letter in some years.

The letter was about my first book. It turns out that some of the story of my journey through a psychiatric ward had resonated with a portion of his own story, so he had written me a really fine letter, one that I now treasure, about what my work had meant to him. I was full of joy from what he said in the letter, full of joy that someone was reading my work, and probably full of myself. I began to tell Father Ed the story of Indianapolis, and the preacher, and the old uncle.

Even though the events of that day in Indianapolis had been so powerful and life-changing for me—and therefore so personal and poignant, or maybe precisely because they were—I had never really told the whole story to anyone. There were tears in my eyes at the remembering and a crack in my voice in the telling. I was just walking along, talking about the importance of that day, about the story of the old uncle in Ireland, about the clarity of the Gospel, and about the mystery of the voice that I had heard all those years ago in Indianapolis. I was lost in the telling of the story, and it took a few minutes before I realized that I was no longer walking with Father Ed.

I have teenagers at my house, so I am used to being ignored while I tell long stories. Father Ed, however, is certainly no teenager, so I was annoyed to find that he was no longer listening to me or even walking beside me. When I turned around to look for him, I discovered he was standing dead still in the middle of the road some considerable distance behind me.

Remembering how Father Ed had been struggling with his health in those days, I was afraid that something was amiss. I rushed back to see if he was okay, vowing that if he would just not die on my watch then I would become a monk after all. When I reached him, he gave me my word.

"That was me," he said.

"Who was you?" I said.

"I was the priest and that is my story. That was my old Irish uncle and that was my trip to Ireland–I was the one who first told that story. I told it because it was my uncle."

I was taken aback because Father Ed was not the one whom I heard tell the story that day in Indianapolis.

I learned months later that the recovering Roman Catholic priest I met in Indianapolis, at a critical moment in his own journey, had wandered his way into a hall to hear a sermon from a priest who turned out to have been Father Ed. The story that he heard that night, the story that he told when I wandered into the back of his room that day in Indianapolis, had been just as powerful to him as it had been to me. It had been powerful enough to lift him up from a life that was coming apart and into a new life, which was the life that had led him to be on pulpits and stages like the one where I heard him in Indianapolis. The story had been so powerful to him that he was still telling it all those years later.

In the divine and mysterious ways that God works in our lives, that story of the old Irish uncle and the telling of it had linked the three of us together over the miles and the years and the stories of our lives.

※※※※※※

I do not know what we are afraid of when it comes to people whose Christian traditions and doctrines are different from ours. I do not know if our fears come from the people who are in charge of our Church institutions or if we generate them ourselves. But I do know that we have a tendency to stay away from, and sometimes look askance at, Christians whose practice is different from ours.

Perhaps we are afraid that if we hang around with them, we will discover practices that will lead to our splitting things up even more, though I am not certain that it is possible to split up the Church further. It makes me think of detailed baseball statistics. I keep expecting to come across a sign posted for a church that reads THE FIRST CHURCH OF THE LEFT-HANDED BELIEVERS WHO ONLY READ FROM THE NEW REVISED STANDARD VERSION ESPECIALLY WHEN THERE IS NO RAIN IN THE FORECAST. We can hardly split up individual churches much more than they are already. Something like 85 percent of Christians go to church in places where fewer than a hundred people attend the church on a regular basis.

It might be that we are afraid that if we talk to each other, we will discover that some people like to sing more than three hymns in a worship service from time to time, or that singing praise choruses with your hands in the air can become just as much an empty ritual as any liturgy ever was. It is possible that we are afraid we will learn that Anglican priests are just as serious about their walk with the Lord as evangelical pastors, or that people from the Church of Christ are just as serious about making sure that relief supplies get sent to the developing world as are mainline liberal folks. Perhaps we are afraid that we will learn that liturgical communities read and sing and say more scripture in an average worship service than many self-described Bible-believing communities will hear from the pulpit in a month of Sundays. Or perhaps we are afraid we will discover that what binds us together is stronger than what has been keeping us from each other.

∞∞∞∞∞

After many years on my journey toward God, I reached a moment in my life at which I wanted to know more about what it meant to live a prayerful life—something I am still discovering (and, alas, am still in no danger of living out all the time). At that very moment, I was introduced to a Southern Baptist religion professor who pointed me in the direction of a former United Methodist pastor who invited me to participate in the Academy and learn some of what the ancient monastics had to say about such a life. It was there that I met and became friends with the Catholic priest who turned out to be the man who first told the story of the old Irish uncle. It was that story I heard repeated by a recovering Roman Catholic priest whose own life was saved by the story, and who spends his life now as an itinerant preacher.

Such a circle—a circle of love and friendship and grace and joy—is not made by accident; it is made by divine conspiracy. Such a circle is not made at all if any one of those in the circle are afraid to talk to the others for fear of being led astray.

I would be nowhere at all on my journey were it not for each member of that particular and rather odd collection of veterans who had traveled the road before me. And were it not for the point of view and the experience and the wisdom that each brought to bear on my journey, I would still be without the light that they shed on me in my darkness.

It is a mysterious thing to me, full of wonder and of grace, and at least part of the mystery is this: A fair number of people that I know, all too often the ones who are in charge of things, the ones who write the reviews, the ones who organize the institutions, and the ones we count on to lead us, would have told me to stay away from all the rest.

Some would have said that these men had no light to offer. Some would have said that these men were theologically dangerous. Some would have said that these men were something less than true believers and true followers of the Christ. In doing so, they would have been wrong. They would have condemned me to live my life on so-called firm theological footing, and to live something less than the life abundant that the Gospel proclaims.

I get to have lunch once a month or so with the dean of the cathedral that I attend. We talk about baseball. I think he likes to have lunch with me for other reasons, too, but I know for certain that he likes me because I can talk baseball. We seldom talk about deep theological issues, unless the World Series includes the Mets or the Yankees.

Every once in a while, however, deep spiritual things do come up. I do not recall the whole conversation, but one day, however it happened, he said to me, "What is the opposite of love?"

I did not reply right away. Hate seemed the obvious answer, but I had the feeling that answer was not going to fly. I was right. "Fear," he said. "Fear is the opposite of love."

"This is how they will know that you love me," said the One Who came among us, "that you love one another." And sometimes that begins with not being afraid of one another.

You cannot love those you fear. And we are called to love. Be not afraid.

7

OVER THE RIVER AND INTO THE WOODS

The Spirit of God joins with our spirit in testifying

that we are God's children.

−SAINT PAUL

———

O God, thou hast made us in thine own image

and redeemed us through thy Son:

Look with compassion on the whole human family;

take away the arrogance and the hatred which infect our hearts;

break down the walls which separate us;

unite us in bonds of love;

and work through our struggle and confusion

to accomplish thy purposes on earth;

that in thy good time all nations and races may serve thee

in harmony around thy heavenly throne;

through Jesus Christ our Lord. Amen.

−THE BOOK OF COMMON PRAYER

WHEN I WAS GROWING UP and it was time to go over the river and through the woods to Grandmother's house for the holidays, I always felt cheated.

A fair amount of the time, one set of grandparents slept over at our house on Christmas Eve, so they were there when we woke up. My journey to see them was little more than over the edge of the bed and down the stairs and through the hallway into the living room.

The trip to see my other grandmother did not take much longer. I could stand on the porch behind our living room and see whether or not she was working in the garden at her house. On Christmas Day, the trip to her house with its big living room and the decorated tree and the freshly squeezed orange juice and the sweet rolls and all my cousins took about the same amount of time that it takes to walk the length of a football field. I did not even get to pass through any woods, either, because my father and brother and I had helped my grandfather clear the ten acres or so where we all lived.

But these days, when the Christmas holidays are upon us, I finally get to go over the river and through the woods. It is the only way to get to David's house.

As far as I am concerned, my friend David throws the best party of the year in this town. It is always held on the first Friday night that follows the local schools' being let out for Christmas holidays. We mark it on our calendar as soon as the school schedule is set every summer, so that we can be sure not to book something else on that day. For me, David's party is where Christmas begins.

I really do have to go over the river and through the woods to get to David's house, which is a long way from where I live. We go north and west of the city up the interstate highway, and then when we have cleared the lights of the city and the suburbs, we come to an exit at the top of the ridge and turn left. Then right at the four-way stop that sits in front of Bubba's gas station. Then we go out on the two-lane state highway in the dark for several miles, and start down a long hill that leads to a small river that feeds into the big one that we crossed when we left town. Just before we get to the bridge, we turn right off the highway and start through the woods. After we wind around through the woods for a little bit, we take the left fork (taking the right fork will send you to Kentucky, I think). In a few yards, we start to see cars parked along both sides of the road.

We park the car and walk toward the house, which is all lit up and shining in the dark. Through the windows, I can see old friends whom I have not seen since last year's party, and there are also usually some new faces among them. There are always some who have been away for a while and are back in town now for one reason or another. All of a sudden, it feels like we have entered a scene from a Hallmark card and come home for the holidays.

The party unfolds in three acts. The first is that you eat and catch up on the news, which is what you always do first at a good party.

The last act of the evening is the dancing—a lot of David's friends can dance well. For a long time, I was afraid that being a good dancer was one of the qualifications for attending, and I was not certain how I sneaked under the radar. Now I go dancing once a year, at David's at Christmas, whether I need to or not. The guests who leave early, and there are some, are leaving too soon, whether they dance or not.

So in the beginning at David's party, you eat and you talk and you greet old friends, some of whom you only see that one time every year. At the end, you dance, sometimes well, more often badly even if enthusiastically.

In the middle, the angels come. Honest, they do—every year—I have heard them.

When I was young and we would go over the patio and through the yard to Grandmother's house, it was almost certain that there would not be any dancing, whether it was

Christmas or not. My family is not the dancing kind, unless they happen to win at Rook.

We had other traditions at Christmas, such as my grand-father's reading from Mark Twain or from collections of po-etry that he loved. He would sit in an armchair with green upholstery and a shell-shaped back, and prop his feet up on an ottoman as his annual performance of "The Cat and the Painkiller" story from *The Adventures of Tom Sawyer* would send us into gales of laughter. "Don't say it unless you mean it, now"–Tom's admonition to the cat whose curiosity was about to get the better of him–is still a kind of all-purpose warning used among my siblings.

My grandfather's reading was the closest we ever came to a collective and focused moment together around word or story at my family's annual Christmas gathering. I have a recollection of having heard the Christmas story according to Luke a time or two at such a gathering, but it does not hold the same place in my memory as did the gospel ac-cording to Mark Twain.

Sometimes he would read from the Mrs. Minerva stories or from Langston Hughes. He had an ear for the dialect and rhythms of African-American speech. Like many middle-class white men in the South in those days, he employed black men on a regular basis to work in his yard and on the houses that he built. I assume that is where that ear for di-alect came from.

If he had close friends who were a different color than us, I never knew about it. He was born around the turn of the nineteenth century, grew up in the Jim Crow South, and lived through the Civil Rights era and then well into the last half of the twentieth century. The patterns of racial relations that allowed for and then promoted more equal contact with people of color never really had a chance to take hold in him. Such things are still taking hold in a lot of us, in fact, not just in my family but in countless families in the South, and everywhere else if the truth be told. Geography is only one of the long list of things that can keep people apart for years and years and years.

I have very fond memories of being at my grandfather's house on Christmas, but I do not remember angels visiting, not the way they come and visit at David's.

I have never been able to pinpoint the angel signal at David's, but there must be one. Whatever it is, the sign is given, then we all begin to put our plates away and start to gather in the living room. We crowd in the doorways, and back into the hall, and into the kitchen. Little songbooks full of holiday songs are handed out, their covers decorated with images of old art from the fifties. There are usually more people than songbooks, so if you don't get one, you stand next to someone who has one.

David's friend Rocky will warm up the organ a little bit—or maybe it is the crowd he is warming up—by noodling around on it.

"O, little town of Bethlehem," we sing, quietly at first until our voices gain in confidence, "how still we see thee lie."

The first trick to really enjoying this part of the party is to be sure that you are standing next to Dan or Paul or David or Donna or Sara or Bev. Or next to someone who is a member of one of the big choirs at the big fine churches downtown. If you are going to sing in public at Christmas or at any other time, be wise enough to stand next to someone who can actually sing; this will help to make you sound as though you can sing as well. Otherwise, when it is time for the glory in the highest, you will sound like me, more like something the shepherds were keeping watch over by night.

The second trick to really enjoying this moment is to be positioned toward the front of the room so that you can stand sideways and watch everyone's faces.

"Once in David's royal city," we sing, at which point some of us invariably find David and grin. He is not the royal David, to be sure, but after singing about three or four songs, those old songs that pull at your heart, you are almost certain that you are standing in some place of nobility, if not exactly royalty. The faces begin to shine back at you.

Across the room is the schoolteacher who has been divorced since the last Christmas party and the woman who has changed jobs three times in twelve months. There is the choir director who has been struggling since the new minister came and his place in the order of things has changed. There are two people holding hands, the two who found each other here last year and who have been together ever since.

There are people of color and people like me, people without much color at all, who may well be less interesting for it. There is the young man who had to tell his brother he could no longer be in business with him, and the one whom my mother once called in the middle of the night when she was in pain and needed help and all her family was out of town. There is a new face or two to the scene, ones that you knew when they were just a child, and now here they are standing before you all grown up. There is the one who just lost a parent and the one who is bearing a burden that you are not certain you could bear even if you tried.

At first, you are struck by how much we are strangers. The crowd is black and white, married and single, young and old, rich and poor, churched and unchurched, devout and whatever the opposite of devout is. ("Not overly pious" is what a friend of mine likes to say.) But then you are moved at how much you are like them.

Two things always astonish me when I stand in that crowd and sing. One is the way that everyone sings those songs. They sing them as though they believe the Story that the songs tell. As though they believe that the Story is true, that the Light of the world is coming, that the arrival of the Light heralds goodwill to all, that there may well be peace on earth, a peace that is not merely the absence of conflict and hatred and strife but a peace that is the presence of something holy and astonishing, something deep and wide, something akin to the Gospel that is proclaimed by the night of the Child itself. They sing these songs as though this is their story, too. It is not like hearing the songs sung in church; it is like listening to the heavenly host.

Which leads me to the second thing: Half the crowd is gay. Where I grew up, and where David grew up, the Story was not meant for such folks—except for the parts about judgment, of course.

⫘⫘⫘

I have some good friends who live a few hours to the east. They are part of a large church. The last time that we were together, they told me that their church was leaving the denomination, or at least it looked that way. The voting was about to take place, and they would know the results in a few days. Because they are all involved in leadership positions in the church, they had been at the center of all the talk and all the prayer and all the decision-making. It had been a hard few months for them. The issue that they were wrestling with in their congregation and in their denomination was whether or not women could be, or should be, allowed to be in the pulpit.

On a business trip to Louisville, I met a woman who knew my friends because she attends a sister church not too far from the one that my friends attend. We talked about them for a minute the way that you do when you discover that you have mutual friends. She asked me if I knew about the choice they were grappling with. I told her that I had heard a little about it.

She acknowledged that it was a difficult choice, and then she told me that the people at her church and throughout the denomination were pretty sure they were going to "lose" my friends and their church. She made it sound as though they were wayward in some way because of the choice that they might make. As though a group of people who thought women should be heard were lost, as though the Gospel would prohibit such a thing.

The woman that I met in Louisville is not alone.

At various stages in the life of the Church here in America, good churchgoers who were like me and some others that I know–white, Anglo-Saxon, Protestant males–were pretty sure that Native Americans had no place among us and that murdering them or stealing their land were perfectly legitimate things to do. Next came the immigrants, the Germans and the Irish and the Asians and the rest; over the years, we were able to convince ourselves that they were something less than people, too, at least for a while. Then it was people who were black who had no place in our churches, or our schools, our buses, or anything else. All of these things were done in the name of God and of the Church.

We are dismayed to think that our forefathers felt the way that they did about people from some corner of the world, of some corner of their own town, that was unknown to them. We are embarrassed that our great-grandfathers might well have fought to keep women from voting. We are ashamed to think that someone in our family tree might well have bought and sold people.

The Body of Christ has been diminished by the lack of love that was demonstrated and by the loss of the gifts of those who were excluded. Once the division had been done, the subtraction cannot even be calculated. It has affected the lives of people like me, and you, and our children for generations, and will continue to do so.

Among us church folks there are plenty who think that women should hold no places of authority within the Church, and are very certain about it. There are plenty of people who think that gay people are to be feared and have no place among us. There are some others who still think that "they"–whatever color "they" are and whoever "they" are for this time and place–do not belong with the rest of us in the pews where people "ascribe unto the Lord the honor due his name."

We church folks have been wrong about such things before, sometimes for centuries at a time, and we may well be simply wrong about these things, too.

I have come to believe that any of us who look to exclude rather than include in the name of Christ are missing something. Which of us, which person of which race, color, gender, or orientation, would Jesus not have welcomed? Look at the way that Jesus dealt with the "they" of his day– the poor, the lame, the Samaritans, the shepherds, the fishermen, the tax collectors, the prostitutes, the women, the children. The people in the Gospel stories who really got grilled about whether or not they might enter the kingdom were the pillars of the community, the ones who kept all the rules, the ones who claimed to know all the truth, the ones who seemed to feel entitled to be included.

He ascended into heaven, from where he came, we say about the Christ in our creeds and from our pulpits. "And his kingdom will have no end" is the other part of that line. I believe that it will not have any boundaries, either. And so I believe that the kingdom that is here and now, the kingdom that the angels proclaimed, the kingdom that Jesus taught was among us now, should have no end and no edges, either.

❦❦❦❦❦

If you were to come with me to David's at Christmas, you would hear the heavenly host. And by the time that you had said good-bye to David and to all the rest, by the time the visiting and the singing and the dancing were done, you would have known that you had been in the presence of angels. You would be a little more certain that the Story was indeed for us all, that those who would use the Gospel to exclude others are missing something.

You would be pretty sure, as you made your way home back over the river and through the woods, that the Light of the world had come, or at least had begun to, and that even the darkness in our own hearts will not overcome it forever.

8

CORE BELIEFS

Let us therefore cease judging one another.

—SAINT PAUL

———

O God, thou hast bound us together in a common life.

Help us in the midst of our struggles for justice and truth,

to confront each other without hatred or bitterness,

and to work together with mutual forbearance and respect.

Grant us not to be anxious about earthly things,

but to love things heavenly;

and even now, while we are placed among

the things that are passing away,

to hold fast to those things that shall endure;

through Jesus Christ our Lord. Amen.

—*THE BOOK OF COMMON PRAYER*

A FRIEND AND I ONCE TALKED for some months about doing a book project together. It was to be a project that combined some of our skills as writers with our perspectives as pilgrims and some of our discoveries as readers. We spoke about it several times over the telephone, and then we finally made arrangements for a time when he could be in town and we could go to meet with a publisher who was interested in the work.

All through the morning, I had the sense that now that he was right up to the edge of doing the book with me, my friend was hedging about whether or not he really wanted to do it. He seemed uncertain about it, and his tentativeness began to make me feel uncertain as well. When I finally pressed him about what was holding him back, he launched into a long exposition of all of the reasons why we could not do the book together. In the end, he said, our core beliefs were just too different.

To be fair, there were then, and are still even now, very real differences in the way that we each live out our faith. He is an evangelical, and I have moved in the other direction within the Church over the years. He is likely to describe himself as a conservative, and I call myself a liberal. And on and on and on. We have known each other for a very long time, and there are a whole host of experiences and re-membrances that clearly demonstrate the ways in which we are different.

The things that he talked about that day, the things that are different about us, the things that he declared were too much for us to overcome—our worship styles and traditions, our political preferences, our literary choices, our parenting styles, our lifestyle choices—are all very important things, but in some ways they are no more essential to the defini-tion of our core beliefs than are our differing zip codes.

Are we different from each other because we have dif-ferent worldviews? Are we different from each other be-cause we have different takes on things such as the inerrancy of the scriptures, the proper way to perform a baptismal rite, and a whole host of things that no pilgrim anywhere any-time is ever going to completely understand or know for sure anyway? Are we different because of the different things that make us feel at home when it comes to worship and prayer and family and manners and customs and tradi-tions? Of course, those things make us different people.

But at our core, down in the place where both of us have wrestled with our faith in God a time or two and come up somewhere between limping and dancing for joy, we be-lieve essentially the same things about God.

We both believe that God is the One Who made us. We both believe that God sent a son to be among us and to

announce the kingdom that had already come and the kingdom that is still to come. And we both believe that we are
called to that kingdom, and called to help build it, and that
if we are going to do anything at all in the name of doing so,
then we must spend our lives working on answers to our
questions about and trying to live out what it means to be a
disciple of Christ. We both believe that we are not able to do
this alone, but are likely to need the help and counsel and
wisdom of others, both those whom we know and those who
have gone before. We both also believe that whether or not
we do any of those things, whether we do them well and
faithfully or badly and haphazardly, we are both dependent
on the mysterious and undeserved mercy and grace of God.

We are both trying to live our lives as devoutly as we
know how and are able. We both spend our lives doing
work that we believe will somehow be acceptable to the
One Who made us and hopefully even matter in the long
run, and we both have demonstrated a fair amount of willingness to forgo almost any earthly success in order to do so.
We both have a clear sense of our vocations, and we both
believe deeply in those callings.

Those are our core beliefs, I believe, and those are
the things that we each would die for, or at least live for,
and those are the things that should be enough to bind us
together.

It was a difficult morning for us. We have been friends
for a long time. It was not easy for him to say those things
to me and I could tell because there were a lot of tears in his
eyes and much anguish in his voice. There was some of the
same on my side of the table as well.

In the end, he made what turned out to be the right choice for us both, and I am grateful that he did. But I still wonder what might have happened had we chosen to try to do the work based on the things that could bind us to each other, rather than to walk away from it based on the things that can keep us from each other.

It took me a long time to figure out what it is that still troubles my heart about what happened. I have finally come to see that it is this: After all the miles and years and shared experiences, after all the things that he and I had done in our lives in the name of trying to live out the Gospel itself, we still only managed to talk about the set of things that could be used to keep us apart.

❧❧❧❧❧

Writers do a lot of things in order to avoid having to write on some days. Reading, for example, which is one of the things that we are doing when we claim to be doing research. While reading a magazine one day, in the midst of an extended period of highly critical research, I came upon an interview with a friend of mine named Eric. He is a very wise man who knows about publishing, and he knows about the Church.

Someone asked Eric to say what he thought about the state of religious publishing today. This is roughly how he replied. (I have to confess that I lost my copy of the magazine long ago, and Eric claims not to remember having said it, but I think it gets better every time that I tell it.)

"For the last five hundred years or so," he said, "one part

of the Church has held the scriptures in trust for the rest of the Church." He was speaking of the Protestant part of the Church. It was that part of the Church, in the years after the Reformation, that was responsible for the translation of the scriptures into the language of the people, making it possible for more and more of us to read and study the Bible.

But in that same period of time, Eric went on, "another part of the Church has held in trust the liturgy and the sacraments for the rest of the Church." Here, he was speaking of the Catholics, the Orthodox, the Anglicans, and the other parts of the Church in which the ancient ways of worship and devotion are still revered and still practiced. "We are living in a time," he concluded, "when people are beginning to ask if they can see what the others have in their box."

It occurred to me that we are not in separate churches but instead are sitting on the same pew, just scattered along it in different places.

❧❧❧❧❧❧

People call me from time to time and ask me to come to lead a retreat or speak at some gathering that they are having. I always get anxious when it is time to go. I am never happy about being away from home, and I am always worried that I am not going to know nearly as much as the people who invited me are hoping that I will know.

The things that I have been learning and writing and talking about—the meaning and practice of the ancient traditions of Christian prayer, the role and power of liturgical and sacramental practice, the history of those things and the ways that they can shape our inner life and our outward journey—have been discussed and wrestled with for a long time at the end of the pew at which I now sit. But at the other end of the pew, the one where my journey began, they have not been.

Oddly enough these days, most of the invitations that I receive to come and speak are from people who are on the end of the pew that I came from, not from the people who sit a bit closer to the end where I am. I do not know exactly why this is so, but I am beginning to feel more comfortable with it as time goes by. (However, there are those who say that I have wandered off into what I was once taught was a far country.)

In some ways, it is like going home again. There is something about that that I really like. There is also something about that that scares me to death.

What makes me nervous is that the listeners will be disappointed. I worry that they will see only the things about us that are different and will not be able to see the things that bind us together. It has happened to me before. It is hard to believe, but sometimes people invite me without having read my books.

Some years ago, I was given what felt to me like a litmus test after I had spent a few days teaching about prayer at a conference on the West Coast. On the third or fourth day, I ended up in a conversation with the person who had issued the invitation. It turned out that the conversation had been arranged in order to call me to task about some of the things that I had said in one of the sessions.

From the inviter's perspective, those things seemed to have raised some question as to whether or not I believed in Jesus Christ and whether or not I thought that Christ was the Son of God. Since I did not use the same language as she did to try to describe my relationship with the One Who came among us, she was not sure that she could be sure that we were talking about the same being. The conversation raised questions in my own mind about whether or not I had written the book very well and whether or not she had read it. It made me sad to think that we were standing there in the parking lot on a fine late-summer day, both of us trying very hard to be good followers of the Christ, and we were talking past each other.

I was taken aback by the grilling. In the course of that week, I had had a sense for the first time in a while of being welcomed and accepted by a group of people with whom I differ theologically in some ways yet share the same sense of calling to bear witness to the One Who made us all and the One Who was sent. It had been a rich time for me spiritually, a homecoming of sorts, and I had been really glad that I had overcome my fears and said yes. As this particular conversation went on, though, it became clear to me that the things that we had in common were not enough to outweigh our differences, that I would not be invited back, and that she was sneaking up on becoming pretty unhappy about having invited me in the first place.

One of my brothers is a pastor, and he and I do not always see eye to eye on theological issues. We like to spend time with each other when we can, to laugh and tell stories and play golf and shoot hoops and tease each other and everyone else in the room. He is warm and funny and has the biggest heart of practically anyone that I know. But on a fair number of the occasions when we have talked about religion, it has been easy for the conversation to become strained. From time to time, we have likely hurt each other's feelings more than we know.

One of the things that we have in common, and I think that we both recognize in the other, is that our spiritual journeys are the most important thing in our lives. Many other things matter to us a great deal, but most everything that we do is seen in the light of our journey home to God.

Ten or twelve years ago, it turned out that we were both staying at our mother's house for a few days. No wives, no children, no other siblings–just the three of us. My mother loved it. She had her two "big boys" at home again and all to herself, and she was pretty much basking in the glory of it. So were we. It had been a long time since we had had such a time to simply enjoy each other's company. There have been times in our lives when it seemed as though the distance between my brother and I has been much farther than the miles that separated our two houses. It happens to all brothers and sisters, I expect.

One morning, during the visit at my mother's, I came downstairs very early. I had fallen behind on something at the place where I was working, and I needed to get to my desk to try and have at it in the hopes that I might make one of the deadlines that I so often missed in those days. When I came around the corner, my brother was sitting at the dining room table, a Bible and another book or two open before him, a journal and a pen within reach, and a cup of coffee in his hands. It was not a surprise to find a pastor at prayer to begin his day, of course, and I knew my brother well enough to know that he had done so for many, many years.

It caught my attention because he was sitting in roughly the same posture that I find myself in most mornings as well, and he had some of the same books and the same tools arranged before him in much the same manner that I arrange mine. I confess that I stood in the hallway and watched him for a few moments without his knowing that I was there. I hated to interrupt him, but he and I had talked about trying to have lunch together that day, and he was to leave town in the evening. I was afraid that the day would get busy and that he and I might miss our lunch because we had not made a plan.

I do not know how it started exactly, this conversation that he and I had that day, but some hours later we were both still sitting there, talking about prayer. Unbeknownst to the other, we each had begun a journey in the direction of a deeper prayer life some years before. We had each managed to survive a number of twists and turns and had come out at roughly the same place at the same time. Because of the miles and the other bits of business that kept us apart, we hadn't realized that we had become brothers in another way, a way that we had not really thought of before, a way that we had never noticed in all the years that we ever talked about religion.

Without our knowing it until that morning, we had been engaged in one of the things that binds us, rather than one of the things that keeps us apart. The prayer itself had made us brothers more deeply when our theological certainties or doubts might well have worked together to make us strangers.

I received a note in the mail from a man in Knoxville, asking me if I could lead a retreat for a dozen or so other men who had been praying and journeying along together for years. He referred to his group as the Mars Hill Dinner Club, so named because they would have dinner together each time there was a new edition of the *Mars Hill Review,* a rightfully highly regarded Christian literary and arts magazine. He also told me that they had been passing around a couple of my books. Flattery may not get you everything, but it can sometimes get you a retreat leader on short notice.

As we swapped notes and telephone calls for a few weeks, and I found out a bit more about them and the church they are from, I became surprised that they called me. Although I am always surprised when anybody calls me, I was also surprised because there was some distance, at least on paper, between the theological positions of their church group and the theological positions of mine. There was some considerable distance between their spot on the pew and the place that I sit. With the memory of my West Coast litmus test still pretty fresh—as was the wound that it had caused—I had my doubts, but by then I had already said yes.

I was nervous as usual when I went to lead the retreat. I wanted as much as anything for them to be happy with the weekend and with our time together. I wanted them to feel as though the time had been helpful to them on their journey, both as individuals and as a group.

We said the daily office together each day, the ancient daily prayers that are rooted in the Christian monastic tradition. We took Communion together each day, and we wrestled with the wisdom for the spiritual life that can be found in the ancient monastic Rule of Saint Benedict. We tried to help each other learn to pray, and we spent long hours in silence and reflection together, listening as attentively as we could and trying to hear what God was saying to us at that particular moment in our journeys.

My fears turned out to be completely unfounded. The Mars Hill Dinner Club group are among the finest people that I have ever known. They were open and honest and attentive and gracious in the face of a whole lot of things they had never experienced.

The first retreat led to another and another, and to a whole series of letters going back and forth between us, then later to a chance to visit their church. It also led to an astonishing gift that they have given to me, over and over again.

One morning not too long after our first retreat, one of the Mars Hill guys called me to say that three or four of them were to be in Nashville the next day, and they were wondering if I would like to have lunch. It sounded to me as though they were passing through and were going to stop to eat lunch anyway and would I care to join them. Because I spend a fair amount of my life in a little room with only a fountain pen and blank paper and some books for company, there are days when the page is not much of a friend and I am grateful for any reason to abandon it to its own devices in order to be around actual human beings. So I said yes.

On the way over to the restaurant to meet them, I confess that I started putting on my retreat-leader air, assuming that some deep issue about prayer or spirituality had arisen among them since our retreat, and that they were feeling the need to speak with me about it. It is easy for some writers to get caught up in their writing, spending way too much time alone and losing what little bit of perspective that they have. I am among the guilty from time to time, more often than I care to know, probably.

When I arrived, we ate lunch together and caught up on the news, but I kept waiting for this big thing to surface. They asked questions about what I was writing next, and we talked about that for a while. Then they asked me about my kids, and I bragged about them for a while. Then they wanted to know about where I was going to speak next and what I was going to say, so I pontificated about that for a bit. Then they asked me how my spirits were and we talked about that. Soon, dessert was done and the coffee was, too, and they said to me that it was time for them to get on the road.

"Where are you guys headed?" I asked.

"Oh, I have to get back to work. I have a staff meeting this afternoon," said one of them. The others murmured about appointments and school ball games and dinner engagements.

"I thought you guys were on the way to somewhere," I said.

"No, we just wanted to see you, see how you were getting along, and make sure you were okay."

Then they hugged me, piled back into their car, and drove the 180 miles home.

These impromptu get-togethers have happened a few more times since then. For some reason that I cannot understand or explain, these guys have adopted me, and from time to time they will drop what they are doing and drop in on me. One of them is a pastor in the very large church that they all attend, another one has a large dental practice, and another owns a civil engineering firm. They all have busy lives and they all have plenty of better things to do than spend a day driving on the interstate to have lunch with me.

I have begun to consider their coming to see me as an act of prayer. I asked them once if they were getting missionary points from their denomination for coming to visit an often-uncertain Episcopalian. They are not, of course; they have just decided that we belong to each other.

We are not bound together by dogma or doctrine or form or denomination. Indeed, if you lay down a list of the things that describe the ways that we live our lives, and the ways that we live out our faith, it would be easy to make a case that we are too different to even be terribly tolerant of each other. Some would say that our core beliefs are not the same at all. Some would advise us to be careful around each other, that our use of such different words to describe our faith is a sign that we are not really brothers. Some would say that we certainly are not on the same pew or maybe even in the same building.

We are bound together because we are trying to learn to pray, because we are trying to learn to listen for the voice of the One Who made us and the One Who came among us, and the One Who will lead us into all truth and eventually lead us home. We are bound together by our willingness to honor one another's witness to that voice in all that we do.

We are bound together because we have begun to realize that a part of our work as members of the Body of Christ is to honor one another's attempts to be faithful, recognizing our brotherhood even as we acknowledge our differences. We are bound to one another because of our core beliefs.

9

THE LIFE TO COME

I am convinced that there is nothing in death or life,

in the realm of spirits or powers,

in the world as it is or the world as it shall be,

in the forces of the universe, in heights or depths—

nothing in all creation

that can separate us from the love of God.

−SAINT PAUL

Almighty God:

We entrust all who are dear to us

to thy never-failing love and care,

for this life and for the life to come,

knowing that thou art doing for them

far better things than we can desire or pray for;

through Jesus Christ our Lord. Amen.

−*THE BOOK OF COMMON PRAYER*

IN THE CATEGORY of close encounters with famous and semifamous persons, I would like to say that I have met Stephen Stills in an airport in Dallas, had lunch with Harry Chapin, and sat two seats away while my son got a baseball autographed by Tommy Lasorda. I also was able to use the players' entrance at Yankee Stadium once, and I have stood on the porch and looked in the window at the hermitage where Thomas Merton used to live. I just wanted you to know that for a shy person, I get around pretty good.

I also once spent three hours and ninety seconds with Henri Nouwen. In many of the circles where people read and think and write about prayer and other spiritual things, Henri Nouwen's name comes up quite a bit. Henri Nouwen is one of the spiritual writers of the past fifty years or so who has written a body of work that has changed a lot of people for the better; has helped to break down some of the barriers between Christians; has opened up many of the deep spiritual traditions and practices that have gone un-noticed in our modern, Western Protestant religious culture;

and, finally, has made it possible for a number of spiritual and religious writers, myself included, to find a platform for our writing and an audience for our books.

Some of us may know only his name, others know his work. The really fortunate among us have known Henri himself. I cannot say, of course, that I really knew him—three hours and ninety seconds is not very long.

He had quite a few friends here in the town in which I live—he had friends everywhere it seems—and so he used to be in and out of town a fair amount. One night, I had the chance to hear him speak. He was wonderful to listen to in public—this thin man with the wild hair and the odd voice and the funny mannerisms and the endearing habit of leading the audience in singing a verse or two of a song as a sort of bridge between the stories he told and the points he made. He spoke for almost two and a half hours that night. And he was so full of life and compassion and gentleness.

Afterward, I was able to meet with him for about ninety seconds. One of Henri's close friends is a man named John, who had been Henri's graduate assistant and then his editor, in a way, for Henri's first few books. As the years had gone by, Henri had become John's mentor, teacher, friend, advisor, and confidant. John and I worked down the hall from each other for a while when I was working in a publishing house, and John became one of my friends, too. That is how he came to take me backstage and introduce me to Henri.

Years later, my wife and I were in New York City. She was in New York to meet with various writers, editors, and agents to see if they might find some publishing projects to do together. I was in New York to carry luggage for her and go out to dinner with her and stay in the hotel with her–which is not bad work if you can get it. (I also have to tell you that you cannot get it. The position has been filled, I have been hired for life, and she has promised not to fire me.)

One of the people she met with that week was Henri. She spent the better part of a day with him and another person or two, talking about projects and possibilities.

In the evening, there was a supper to which a couple dozen people were invited. The agenda for this supper was very different from the meeting of that afternoon.

Henri used to spend a fair amount of time at such informal suppers, raising financial support for L'Arche, a set of communities for disabled people, to which he was attached as chaplain for many years. Whenever he was traveling the world, doing the things that Henri Nouwen, writer and speaker, was doing, he would often spend an evening or a day doing some work to help raise money for Daybreak, the particular L'Arche community where he lived.

I know this because I was invited to the New York City supper, and at one point I found myself in the floor of an apartment that overlooked Central Park. As I sat cross-legged, with a plate of spaghetti on my lap and a glass of wine on the floor beside me, I became engaged in a long and animated conversation with Henri Nouwen. In my limited experience, I would venture to guess that all conversations with Henri were animated.

That night, Henri was full of laughter, talk, fun, and curiosity. We talked books and ideas, told stories, and kept interrupting each other with our laughter and carrying on. At one point, he handed me his plate to hold while he left the room to go dig in his luggage for a book that he was reading. He wanted to read a paragraph to me to make a point, and it turned out that we were reading the same obscure little prayer book at the same time. I told him that my copy was in my bag in my hotel room, and we shared more laughter about that.

The best part of the experience for me that night was to find that Henri was absolutely transparent, that there was not much distance at all, if any, between the Henri Nouwen who was revealed on the pages of his books or in his presence on a stage and the Henri Nouwen who was sitting cross-legged on the floor across from me. He was honest and true and alive and whole and himself. It was easy to see why people thought of him as one of God's favorites.

✦✦✦✦✦✦

A few springs ago, on a cold and rainy Wednesday, I saw a photograph in the *New York Times* of a young woman, her niece, and her nephew as they stumbled across a cold and wet border into a place called Macedonia. Her brother had not been allowed to come with them; he had been killed. The authorities in Bosnia and Herzegovina were not taking any chances that anyone who was a male and in his mid-thirties might live to fight another day.

On Thursday, I received a telephone call about my brother Tom, the one who it seems was ultimately "too gentle to live among wolves," as James Kavanaugh once described a friend of his. It was the telephone call that told those of us who loved Tom that he was gone, and by his own hand it turned out.

On Friday, I went to the cathedral where I attend Good Friday services each year, and it was difficult to listen to the reading of the story of the final moments of the One Who is our Brother as well as our Redeemer. If we are to be joint heirs with him, fellow sons and daughters of God himself, then the story of his death on the cross is the story of the death of our Brother, and we were there among his sisters and friends beside his mother at the foot of that cross. And thinking of our Brother and my brother both lying in a tomb on that Friday afternoon was almost more than I could bear.

On Saturday, I was at a funeral home that some of our old family friends own, a place where people gather in order to begin to say good-bye to people whom they love. I took another of the steps along the way to say good-bye to my brother Tom, the journey that had begun for us on the afternoon when we heard the news.

I saw an old friend that evening who had just buried his brother the day before, and he and I agreed that it had been a hard week for those who love their brothers from here to Macedonia and back. I knew then, in my head at least, that our sorrow would someday be turned to joy, and I was willing to vote for it being sooner rather than later, but it had not happened at that time—and it may not have happened yet to some of us, no matter what any of us have said in the years that have gone by.

This is one of the sentences that is read in the Old Testament lesson in the Episcopal service on Good Friday: "Out of his anguish, we shall see light."

There must have been plenty of anguish surrounding Tom that afternoon up in the rough country on the other side of Monteagle Mountain, down toward the southeast corner of Tennessee.

There was enough anguish that it spilled out horribly down that mountainside, along with his very life and breath, and down across the miles and trees and rocks and ridges until it settled onto all of us–his mother and his brothers and his sister and his two good children and the people that loved him most and best. None of us–despite what was said at the time in the name of comfort and consolation–were capable of going from sorrow to joy, from loss to triumph, from anguish to light in those days.

Tom was too young and too good-looking and too funny and too dear to all of us for that to happen. His anguish became our own somehow and left us looking desperately for the light that has been promised.

It was around the time of Tom's death that we heard the news that Henri had died. We learned about it at our house when we caught the tail end of a memorial piece on the radio. He had been in Holland, which was his home, to visit some of his family. He had had a heart attack, and over the course of a few days, he had gone from seemingly healthy to critically ill to rallying for the better to turning for the worse to death. I called my friend John as soon as I heard the news. I knew that John would be hurting, so I called to try to say what all of us call to try to say but never can really find the words for at such times.

Henri had been buried in Holland near his family, but there was to be a memorial service at Daybreak in Toronto so that his friends there and in the United States could do their best to send him off. John was going, of course.

On the morning of the memorial service, I did something that I had never done before but have learned to do from time to time ever since. At the hour appointed for Henri's service far away in Canada, I went out to my little studio and closed the door. I just wanted to be with John and the others, the ones who had gathered up to say good-bye to Henri. I guess that I wanted to be with Henri as well, although I was hardly a member of his inner circle and I knew few of his precious friends.

I could not afford to go to Toronto, and probably would not have even if I could, but I wanted to add my presence to Henri's friends. I wanted to add my voice to the voices of all the faithful of time past, so to speak, to give thanks for Henri and to participate in the sending off of this good one among us to the place where there are gathered all those who have gone before.

So I sat down on the floor of my studio, I lit a candle and I pulled out *The Book of Common Prayer,* and I turned to the Service for the Burial of the Dead. I read it aloud slowly, with as much reverence as I could muster, inserting Henri's name in the appropriate places and the names of some of

Henri's friends in their places as well–John, Marjorie, Steve, Billy, Jim, Tom, Eric, Alice, and a few more whose names that I knew.

I had never done such a thing before, read the service for the dead, not when my father died or my grandparents or anyone else. I have no idea if laypeople are even supposed to do such a thing. I do not know what bishops or deans or priests would say about my doing so, though I suspect they would say that it is okay.

There is a place in the service, in the moments after the anthems, collects, and lessons have been read, when what comes next is the creed. "I believe in God, the Father almighty, maker of heaven and earth. . . . And in Jesus Christ, the only Son our Lord . . . conceived . . . born . . . suffered . . . died . . . descended . . . rose . . . ascended . . . again . . . the living and the dead . . ." It goes on, and I read it aloud. The words were familiar to me as they are to many of us. "The Holy Spirit, the holy Catholic Church, the communion of saints, the forgiveness of sins, the resurrection of the body . . ."

And then I took a long, deep breath–"the resurrection of the body."

At that point in my life, I was more than forty years along in my journey from one end of the spectrum of Christian faith toward the other end. I had gone from Nazarene to Methodist and on to the Episcopal crowd. I had stood with people like you and with others like us on Sunday after Sunday for many years and had said those words over and over.

By the time I was in my studio saying good-bye to

Henri, I had spent most of the previous ten years on a thoughtful walk in the direction of a deeper and deeper immersion in the traditions, sacraments, and practices of the liturgical part of the Church. I had grown up with Gospel stories as told in every form, from study books to flannel graphs to fiery revival sermons to big-time Christian rock and roll. Now here I was sitting on the floor of my studio, saying prayers for the dead for a funny Catholic priest from Holland whom I hardly knew, in solidarity with a crowd of people that I did not really know, and suddenly I had lump in my throat when I got to the words *the resurrection of the body and the life of the world to come.*

It was not because it was the first time that I had ever heard these words said about someone. I had already buried my father, my grandfather, and others. It was because of something else: For the first time in my life, at a moment when someone was being laid in a tomb, I was required to say what I believed at just such a moment, and as I said it, I suddenly believed it—for the first time perhaps, or at least it felt like the first time to me.

I believe that about Henri, I thought to myself. Henri, who could charm the paint off the wall and bring an audience to tears with his off-key singing of "Ubi Caritas." Henri the companion and Henri the guide. Henri the writer, who may well be among the few of God's witnesses whose work will still be read in a hundred years. Henri cannot be finished for good simply because he is finished here.

Then, it dawned on me: If I believed that about Henri, I could believe it about my father and my grandfather, and my brother, who died too young. And if I believed it about them, I could believe it about others as well, from here to Monteagle Mountain to Macedonia and anywhere else.

Finally, I could believe in the resurrection of the body, even if it is my own. On the days when I can hardly stand and say it aloud for the sake of my own grief or my own burdens or my own pain, on the days when it is difficult to do so for the sake of my own doubts and for the sake of my own sins. On those days, too, I must say what I believe, and say it until it has taken root in me and grown into something that does, indeed, resemble belief.

In the category of going on to other things, Tom, of course, has now gone on to other things, however it all works out theologically. I am not too clear about the details of such things and am inclined to defer to those more learned, but I do know that he is not here, so he must be somewhere. Wherever that is, he is up to something.

I should imagine that he and my father have already torn down the fence and put in a couple new beds and some monkey grass and hostas around the mansion that is being prepared for us. Just because it was previously made for us by some heavenly construction crew would not keep Tom and my father from doing a little work on it.

Tom always knew the secret that my father knew—the secret that my wife knows—that planting something in the ground with your own two hands is an act of prayer, perhaps a more sacred and honest one than any that I have ever said. It is not my favorite way to pray, though I do it sometimes. It still strikes me as being a great deal like manual labor, but my dad and my wife and my brother Tom are not likely to be wrong about such a thing.

My brother Tom has gone. I am not glad that he is gone, but I am glad that he no longer knows the anguish that he knew. It takes a lot of anguish to make a suicide.

I am glad that at least one of the new things to which he has gone is the realization that he was loved far more than he ever really knew here, that he meant more to all of us than he ever really understood while he was here with us, that the world was better for us because he was in it, and that it still is just for the memories of his being with us.

But for those of us who knew Tom, it will take time and effort before we see any light out the window of his anguish. That is true for any of us who remember those "whom we have loved but no longer see," as the prayer book calls them.

I do not completely understand why the stories of these two deaths go together in my mind. On the surface, they are very different.

Henri was a candidate for sainthood for almost all his life, and rightly so. It turns out that Tom was a candidate for suicide much of his life, and tragically so. One died past the halfway point of his life, surrounded by his family, who had a chance to say the things that they wanted to say before he left. The other died far too young and alone, in the dark and

THE LIFE TO COME ◆ 139

the cold spring rain, leaving nothing behind but a note that gave the rest of us a chance to say nothing in return.

In the end, accompanied by the prayers and the presence and the grief and the loss of those who loved them, both were committed to the grave and passed from beyond our sight.

Part of the reason that I think of their deaths together is because I believe in one of the things that Henri taught. "As long as we have our stories," he once wrote, "there is hope." I have come to believe that we must, of course, tell all our stories, even the ones of death and loss. Otherwise, there is a risk that we will forget what we say we believe to be true: that death does not win in the end.

Further, I have come to believe that if we believe those things to be true for the Toms and the Henris and everyone in between, then we have a chance to finally stop looking at one another the way that we do sometimes. We may stop seeing one another only as the dying and start to see each other as among those who are to live forever. It is so easy for us to be judgmental, and we are so quick to be so sometimes, regarding who is headed home to God and who is not.

It is easier to believe that the Henris of the world will live forever than it is for some of the rest of us, to be sure. But if we are going to believe it for Henri, then we have to believe it for the rest of us. Because, as Saint Paul says, there is nothing that can ultimately separate any of us from the love of God anyway.

We can believe it for those who are among the afraid

and the anguished, the sick and the lame, the feeble and the frail, the hard to get along with and the hard to take. We can believe it for the ones who pray the way that we do and for the ones who do not. We can believe it for the ones who are the most like us and the ones who are the most unlike us.

All of them are our brothers and sisters, and not just for now, but for all time to come. It will be easier when we have all been changed, as the old songs tell us that we will be, into someone who is as kind and gentle as Henri and as tall and good-looking as Tom. But either way, we may as well get used to it.

At the Christmas holiday a few months before Tom died, our whole family was together. As was our custom at all large family gatherings, Tom and I spent time outside together sitting on the steps, and we got to talking a bit.

We had not talked in a while. One of those bits of business that come between brothers from time to time had come between us a few months before, so we had been staying clear of each other. I think he was angry with himself about what had happened and more than a little embarrassed; I know that I was angry with myself about it and embarrassed, too. But on the steps that night, we fell to talking, and before too long we were saying we were sorry and trying to figure out how to make amends and go on from there.

At the end of it, as we stood up to head inside, we put our arms around each other and said all that stuff that you say at such times—"I'm sorry," "Please forgive me," "I really love you." At the end, Tom held my shoulders in those great strong hands of his, looked down at me with his twinkling eyes, and said, "You are forgiven, my son, go and sin no more." It was, of course, hysterically funny, and I fell over laughing. So did he.

"The shortest distance between two points," wrote Ralph Keyes, "is a straight line. A straight line like I love you. I need you." Other lines come to me as I think of the one that Tom wrote: "I am afraid. I am lonely. I am scared. I am in despair and anguish."

"Go and sin no more," said our Brother, the One Who came among us, long before my own brother Tom said it to me with a twinkle in his eye—which is a pretty straight line itself, even though my brother used it to deflate the air of tension between us.

Sometimes I think about Tom and Henri and all the others whom I have loved and no longer see, and I wish that I had made some straight lines in their direction before they were gone. Sometimes I think about us all, we who call ourselves the Body of Christ, and I think that it may be time for us to go and say some straight lines.

Go and put your arms around your brothers and sisters. Go say to them that you are sorry about the things that you have said. Go and say that you want to start over.

Go and tell them that you love them.

If we are to see the light that is to come from the anguish

of being apart, then we must find those from whom we are estranged—the loved ones we have not spoken to in weeks or months or years; the friends whose telephone numbers that we no longer call because of some long-forgotten hurt that was never brought into the light and offered up to a brighter light; the sons and daughters and mothers and fathers to whom we have offered no invitations or forgiveness or thanks or kindness in far too long.

We must make more room for those who are different from us, not less room. We must learn to greet each other as brothers and sisters—and not just the ones who look like us, act like us, think like us, and theologize like us. We must make peace with the others on the pew from whom we have been estranged for so long, and whom we have been so quick to judge.

If we are to see the light that is promised to us, the light that is promised to us out of the anguish of our Brother, we must seek out his brothers and sisters, all of them, and offer up some straight lines.

10

WALKING THE BEACH

Let love for our brothers and sisters
breed the warmth of mutual affection.

–SAINT PAUL

———

All praise and thanks to thee, most merciful God,
for adopting us as thine own children,
for incorporating us into thy holy Church,
and for making us worthy to share
in the inheritance of the saints in light.
Grant us, we pray, all things necessary
for our common life,
and bring us all to be of one heart and mind
within thy holy Church;
through Jesus Christ our Lord. Amen.

–*THE BOOK OF COMMON PRAYER*

"WHEN THE GOING GETS TOUGH, the tough get going" goes the old saying. I would add that it is best if you get going to the beach. The truth is that I try to get going to the beach twice a year, whether the going is tough or not. I figure one should probably go just in case.

One of those two times each year is when our wedding anniversary comes around and the two of us, just the two of us, go to the beach to celebrate. We usually go to the same beach in southern Alabama, partly because it is the closest beach within driving distance of our front door, and partly because it is always deserted by the time we go in late October. And we like that.

We pretty much just hole up in a little house, lay in a stack of provisions, and read books and take naps and lie in the sun and take more naps. On some days we get off the deck that overlooks the Gulf of Mexico, and on some days we do not. Some days we see another person or two, and some days we do not even look.

Our rule for the week is "one thing a day," something I learned about going to the beach from my brother-in-law. If I am to cook that day, then I do not do another thing. If it is my turn to run to the market, then I do not have to make the bed. One thing each day that looks like work or activity, and that is all. Driving to the little restaurant at the marina so someone else can cook or opening the beach umbrella if the sun is too hot do not count as actual things.

I always get up early, even when we are at the beach. My wife thinks that early rising would count as her one thing if she had to do it, but I do not see it that way for me.

In the first place, I cannot help myself. I have been rising early for many years now, first as part of a prayer discipline that I shared with some friends for a while, then as a way to begin to write sentences before my brain became too filled with daily stuff, and then as a time for writing in my journal. It is now a combination of all three, plus other stuff, too—drinking coffee, trying to get my eyes to focus, and tidying the house a little because such work always goes faster early in the morning than it does just before bedtime.

I have come to a place in my life where I enjoy watching the sun come up, and there is no place better for that than the beach. So even at the beach, I will set an alarm (the only thing one is allowed to use a clock for while on vacation). Most beach mornings will find me sitting in a folding chair down on the sand, wrapped in a blanket and nursing a cup of coffee, and scribbling in a journal or scratching notes in the margins of a book while waiting for the sun to rise and the sky to go from black to red to blue.

I like to listen to the hum of the fishing boats as they return from their night's labors, and I enjoy the screech of the shorebirds as they fly low along the water into the sunrise, doing their own fishing. There is always the sound of the surf, of course. The comfort of it keeps your mind and spirit gently rolling in time to the rhythm of the world as God says let there be light once more.

※※※※※※※

While at the beach one year, I was reading Saint Paul's letters. He said many things that I do not understand, and much of what he said has been twisted around into theological and ideological statements and positions that separate Christians from each other. Saint Paul said a lot of things that even my friend the Answer Thomas cannot wrestle all the way to the ground for me.

I was looking for what Saint Paul had to say about what it is that makes us a community, about what he had to say about those of us who would follow him into this thing that we call the Church, about the way we are to live together so that we might become the Body of Christ. I was looking for what he said that might unite us rather than divide us. I had been to various places in the few months before our beach trip, where it was clear to me that some people in the Church are actively engaged in keeping us from each other, and they had quoted Saint Paul to justify the divisiveness.

I have been around the scriptures and the study of it all

my life—long enough to be aware that you can use the scriptures to back up your position on just about anything that you want to. You can outlaw women in pulpits, put them in charge of Sunday school classes, and keep them from talking, all by quoting from the same set of verses. You can outlaw divorce, justify it in some contexts, and make a case for no marriage at all, finding justification for each within the space of just a few verses. You can throw people out of a congregation, welcome others back in who have made the same mistakes that the ones who you threw out just got through making, and make a case for having shown mercy to both sets, and you can do so with a straight face, if you want to. A fair amount of that ecclesiastical juggling can be traced to the writings of Paul.

So I set out to read him, to read him as a grown-up, or at least as much of a grown-up as I seem to be able to pretend to be.

I started with a recently purchased hardback edition of *The New English New Testament*. It is my favorite translation. Just the sheer poetry of it moves me. Because it is out of print now, I buy copies whenever I run into them in used-book stores. I am embarrassed to say how many I have bought over the years.

With a fountain pen in my hand, I set out to copy into a little notebook the things that Saint Paul said about how we are to treat each other, we who are to be the Body of Christ. For the purposes of the exercise, I skipped over all the history parts, descriptions, and great theological explanations of the Gospel. I did not do so because those things are not

important, but because they did not seem relevant to the
question that I had on my mind.

Such an approach to reading and interpreting the scriptures makes some people very nervous. Some call it proof-
texting. Others are quick to accuse me of just picking and
choosing what I want to hear.

In my experience, we all do that with the scripture much
of the time—at least those of us who have not yet sold everything that we have and given it to the poor do. So do those
of us who have not only taken a knapsack and shoes for the
journey—in contradiction to what Jesus told his disciples to
pack when he sent them off—but armed ourselves with
portable CD players, cell phones, a couple of suitcases, not
to mention the overabundance of stuff in our attics and the
storage units that we rent just to contain it.

The scriptures are a living thing. They are meant to be
wrestled with again and again as best we are able to at a
given point in our journey. Sometimes, that means wrestling
with one line, two lines, or two hundred lines at a time.

Holding all the scriptures in my head, understanding
them, and living them all of the time is about as possible as
completely understanding everything there is to understand
about God in the first place. If I think I am holding the Mystery that is God in my head and heart, it means I may be
worshiping some other thing. That thing may well be a Mystery, but I am careful about using the name God for it. If
Robert can understand it completely, it is fairly certain that
it is not God.

Just before we went south to the beach that year, I had been to the Northwest to a writers' conference. I was there to do a workshop or two about the relationship between one's writing life and one's spiritual life.

The real reason that I went is because my wife was going. She works in publishing as well, as an agent who represents a crowd of writers, and she does so with such great style, wisdom, wit, and ability that she is often asked to attend writers' conferences so that she can share her knowledge. She is also, it is hoped, going to run into some new talent there and help them to begin their career. If the organizers ask her to "do a workshop," her standard reply is that although she does not do workshops, she has a man who does them for her—and that is me. So they invite me as a way to get her to come. It works for me, too, because I do not like to be away from her. I also like to hear myself talk, and it provides an opportunity for me to look literary for a few days, which I try to do at least ten or twelve days a year.

As is often the case, there were many differences between me and the people who by and large attended the Northwest conference. They were looking at God through a different set of windows than I am these days, and sometimes that made it hard for us to find a common language to use to describe our search for and our experiences of the Holy. There were several hundred folks there who were all using the same language, and I was feeling a little left out in the cold. It was no one's fault in particular, it just happened. I have felt *other* my whole life, anyway—most shy, quiet, poetic types do—and I have learned to generally muddle my way through.

One of the times that I felt the most odd was when the group would gather up in the evenings for worship. I am an "evening prayer, liturgy, old hymn" sort of worshiper. These people were "praise choruses, hands in the air, and guitar" sorts of folks. I mean no value judgment in that, it is just the truth about us both. In situations like that, I am always less than comfortable, not because of the way anyone is treating me, or because I think that they are worshiping incorrectly somehow, but because of my own story and my own journey.

When I was younger, I spent ten years working in the Christian music business. To be a good citizen in Nashville, as I understood it, you have to work ten years in the music business to make your civic contribution to the ongoing prosperity of Music City, U.S.A. Then you earn your honorable discharge and go on with your real life. It is easier than military service, but it can leave you unfit for certain things. One of those things for me is singing contemporary Christian music very loudly while clapping your hands and listening to guitars. I simply have been there and done that so many times that it is not a way that I can comfortably worship anymore. Others do, but I cannot. I am certain that God enjoys it but it is hard for me to. It is for God, anyway, and not for me. I try to make other offerings.

When the crowd at the writers' conference gathered up for worship in the evenings, I would find a place in the back so that I could slip out and sit quietly under the sky while the other folks worshiped inside. However, on the last night of the conference, they faked me out, though I do not think that they intended to trick me.

As a way of thanking the published writers who had been teaching workshops and classes, they had arranged for us to sit together in a semicircle on the stage. The ten or twelve of us had a chance to talk for a minute or two about our most recent book and to answer questions from the audience. It was a nice thing for the organizers to do, and when someone wants to give you a chance to look like you are somebody, then you say yes and take your seat up front.

As that part of the evening wrapped up, with all of us still sitting on the stage, a woman with a guitar stood up and started in on the first chorus—I was trapped.

For the next twenty minutes, the crowd sang and clapped together. I kept trying to find something to do with myself so that I would not look so lost that anyone would notice. After a while, I did what I had seen monks do, and that was to just close my eyes with my hands folded in my lap, meditating my way to some distant place and trying for a beatific look on my face. After four or five days around so many other humans, what I needed most was silence, not more noise, even if it was of the joyful kind. So off I went, so to speak.

I thought about all the times that I had sat in such rooms and heard such singing. And I thought about the distance that had been traveled since, and I was grateful for my own journey and for having made it this far to wherever it was I had reached on that day. And then I thought about the things that seemed to separate me from those who had filled up the room around me: theology and worship and practice and politics and language. I was not sure how I felt about all those differences, to be honest.

So I opened my eyes to have a look at them, and I discovered two things. One was that in my few minutes away, contemplating the mysteries of life and such, I had missed an unspoken cue, and everyone in the room was standing now—everyone except me. It is one thing when you are in the back row and another thing altogether when you are on the stage.

The other thing I noticed was that I was looking up into this sea of faces that were shining so brightly and so sweetly that I could hardly bear it. *No wonder God likes these people,* I thought to myself.

So I stood up.

Unlike most of the others, I kept my hands in my pockets; but I stood up so that I could be counted. I want to be in that number.

⚟⚟⚟⚟⚟⚟

Months later, I am at the beach and under the influence of the sound of the sea and the words of Saint Paul. The creation is beginning again; I know this because the sky is turning pink in front of me.

The memory of that moment in the Northwest drifts into my head, and I stand up from my cross-legged position and start to walk along the beach, heading toward the sun along with the shorebirds. I am remembering the words of Saint Paul in my head, and I am seeing those sweet faces and hearing that sweet singing.

I am feeling the weight of all those hands on my shoulders in northern Florida, where those people from that mega-church prayed for me once, and I am recalling the sight of that priest as he sat in our circle in northern Alabama with his eyes closed and his hands in his lap. I am seeing the woman who gave me the litmus test in a different light now, and the ones who cannot share the Table because they are bound by someone else's rules.

I am remembering the Mars Hill Dinner Club as they pull into a restaurant parking lot, and I am thinking of four high school kids walking toward the cafeteria for the FCA meeting. I am watching in my mind's eye as an old Irishman watches the sun come up, and I am praying with Henri's friends and crying with Tom's children.

It comes to me then. It comes to me finally, irrevocably, utterly—I belong to them all, and they all belong to me. Anyone, anywhere, who says otherwise is as wrong as they can be, no matter how well intentioned or thoughtful they happen to be.

We are not of different faiths or different religions—we are Christians, all of us. We are not in different churches; we are in the same Church on different parts of the pew. Some of us are looking mostly through this window or that one, while some of us are on our way to have a look into a window from which the view of the Mystery that we cannot name looks a little different.

The walls that have been built between us—the ones built out of fear or pride or ignorance—can be taken down. And we who sit on this pew must do exactly that. We are the ones who can stop the daily dividing up of the Body of Christ into pieces and, instead, make it more possible for the Christ to be seen in our world.

We must seek out the things that we have in common and at the same time learn to honor the things that make us different. We must learn to take the things that we hold dear—our sense of community, our love for the scriptures, our hunger for prayer, our capacity for worship—and work to make them wide enough and deep enough to include others rather than keep them at a distance.

We must be willing to cultivate humility along with certainty, to practice tolerance along with devotion, to seek patience along with piety.

We must learn to seek the face of the Christ in those who are different as readily as we do in the faces of those who are like us.

We must learn to love one another.

AUTHOR'S NOTES

In a very real sense, a writer works alone. And it is just as true that a writer cannot do his work alone. The whole process, at least for me, nearly always takes the help of a small army of folks who have chosen for one reason or another to be kind and gracious to me and my work.

I am grateful to them, as always, and offer up my gratitude here with a grin on my face and a lump in my throat. I wish that I were poet enough to be able to say just how grateful that I am for their kindness to me.

Thank you to Phyliss, Jim, Geoffrey, and Drew, all of whom agreed to serve as forepersons in the jury for whom this work was written.

And to the kind folks at Mount Hermon, in California, and Christ Church Cathedral, in Nashville, for allowing me to stand in places that are far better than I am and to pinch-hit for the dean, and for their listening to part of the work on this book in its early stages and encouraging me to continue.

And to the people at Doubleday, particularly Eric Major and Michelle Rapkin, who took me in and kept me on. And to the good folks at WaterBrook who made this new edition possible.

And to Ms. Bo of Hendersonville, Ms. Dupree of New York, Ms. Lil of Linda Lane, and Ms. Jones of Merigold—without whom I would be hard-pressed to make any book at all.

※※※※※※

There are a number of sources that I kept turning to over the time that I spent writing this work. I am grateful to the people who wrote them, the people who published them, and to the people who introduced me to them.

The scriptures cited throughout are my own paraphrases, but they are largely based on *The New English Bible* (published by Oxford University Press).

The prayers in this book are adapted from the 1979 edition of *The Book of Common Prayer* (published by the Church Hymnal Corporation) as used by the Episcopal Church of America.

Some portions of the description and explanation of *The Apology of Justin the Martyr* previously appeared in a book that I wrote called *That We May Perfectly Love Thee* (published by Paraclete Press).

Years ago, I was asked to write a short piece for my friend Gloria Gaither for a book she developed called *What My Parents Did Right* (recently reissued by Howard Publishing). I warned her then that I might use some of the material about my father somewhere down the line, and it has finally happened. I am glad that she asked me to write it in the first place.

Finally, my thanks goes to the Friends of Silence and of the Poor and to the members of the Academy Forum, a group of people who have attended the Academy for Spiritual Formation over the years. Their prayers and their encouragement have meant more to me than I can say.

Namaste to you all, *namaste*.

R. Benson
Nashville, December 2002

ABOUT THE AUTHOR

ROBERT BENSON is a writer, retreat leader, and conference speaker who lives in Nashville, Tennessee.

He can be reached by mail at 1001 Halcyon Avenue, Nashville, Tennessee 37204, and he is always happy to hear from fellow pilgrims.